STORIES FOR TELLING

A Treasury for Christian Storytellers

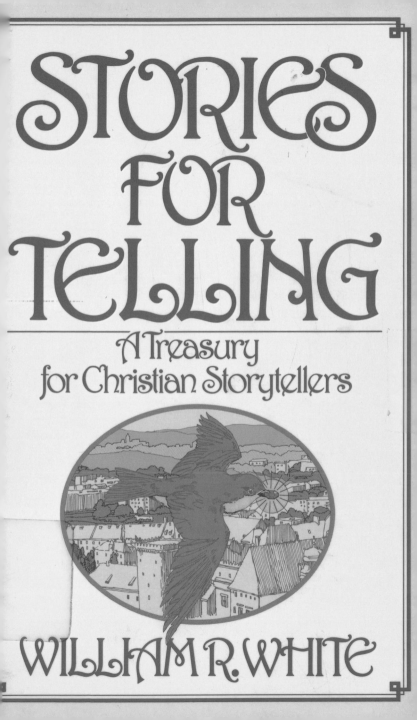

WILLIAM R. WHITE

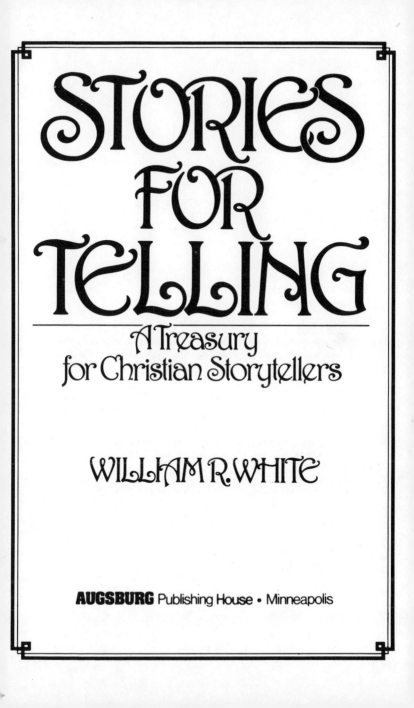

STORIES FOR TELLING

A Treasury for Christian Storytellers

WILLIAM R. WHITE

AUGSBURG Publishing House • Minneapolis

To Sally

STORIES FOR TELLING
A Treasury for Christian Storytellers

Copyright © 1986 Augsburg Publishing House

Scripture quotations unless otherwise noted are from the Revised Standard Version of the Bible, copyright 1946, 1952, and 1971 by the Division of Christian Education of the National Council of Churches.

Scripture quotations marked NIV are from the Holy Bible: New International Version. Copyright 1978 by the New York International Bible Society. Used by permission of Zondervan Bible Publishers.

Library of Congress Cataloging-in-Publication Data

White, William R. (William Robert), 1939-
   STORIES FOR TELLING.

  Bibliography: p.
  1. Story-telling in Christian education.
2. Christian fiction.   I. Title.
BV1534.3.W485   1986   268'.6   85-28980
ISBN 0-8066-2192-3

Manufactured in the U.S.A.   APH 10-6023

1 2 3 4 5 6 7 8 9 0 1 2 3 4 5 6 7 8 9

CONTENTS

3

PREFACE

With rare exception, the stories that follow have all been told by me during Sunday morning worship, in Christian education, or at the Great Lakes Religious Storytelling Festival, held annually in Michigan. The material in the first two chapters, along with many of the tales, was used in a series of church workshops called "Stories to Live By." This, then, is a book that is of and for the church.

These stories were not just prepared for the family of God, they were shaped by that family. The counsel and suggestions of people from my congregation, as well as the advice of friends and colleagues in the church, led to many discoveries and revisions. Three friends and members of my Mount Pleasant church family, Marilyn Zorn, Sally White, and Shelia Dailey, have made valuable contributions to this book. Marilyn and Sally read the entire manuscript and made important suggestions. Shelia, a professional storyteller, introduced me to many of the stories and made corrections that only another storyteller could make. I am deeply grateful for the unique contribution of all three friends.

A number of people who read *Speaking in Stories*, my earlier book, were surprised that I tell the stories a bit differently than

I wrote them. Like other writers who have attempted to put the oral word on the written page (see the preface to Martin Luther King Jr.'s book of sermons, *Strength to Love*), at times I find the two media to be incompatible. I have attempted to stay close to the oral form in this book. Still, the reader who wishes to tell these stories will have to make some minor adjustments.

Although I have collected and adapted all of the stories in this book, I am the original author of only one of them. However, after living with them and telling them for three years, I have come to think of them as mine. As you read and adapt them for your use, I hope that you will consider them yours as well.

1

THE SEARCH FOR TRUE STORIES

The bondage of television

We live in a storytelling age. Television, a device so powerful that it commands how a significant percentage of the nation spends its time, is primarily a storytelling medium. It is so dominant that communication experts estimate that the average person watches 30,000 electronic stories before he or she reaches the age of 21. Like all stories, these electronic tales teach while they entertain. As we sit in front of the "plugged-in-drug," we absorb the values and life-styles that pass before us. The little picture box in our homes has become one of the most influential teachers for both adults and children.

In a sense all television stories are commercials. They urge the listener (viewer) to accept a point of view or to assume a new position. Television sells attitudes, values, and life-styles as well as deodorants and mouthwash.

Though television executives continue to argue that their programs only reflect the values of the country rather than shape them, few students of the media would agree. Critics, such as Professor George Gerbner of the University of Pennsylvania, have shown that television creates its own world and then convinces us that the illusion is true. As anchorman Howard Beale said in the movie *Network*, "You people sit there, night after night. You're beginning to think the tube is reality and your own lives are unreal. This is mass madness."

In the world of television men outnumber women three to one. Violent acts occur 10 times more frequently than in the real world (there are 18 acts of violence per hour on children's weekend TV), most people are employed in white collar or professional jobs, and blacks and minorities are almost invisible. Older people, if present at all, are seen as silly, stubborn, or eccentric.

Marriage, married people, and traditional sexual values are increasingly presented in a negative light on television. Married men are not nearly as big and strong as single men in the world of the tube. Sexual intercourse between unmarried partners is implied or occurs seven times as often as intercourse between a husband and wife. In recent years TV writers have even found it difficult to sustain "interesting stories" about people who have healthy marriages. The solution, as in the case of the series "Rhoda," is to arrange a quick TV divorce.

Although those who study the impact of television on the lives of people are not in total agreement, there is increasing evidence that we are strongly influenced by the stories we watch. Two recent studies of television concluded that the more television viewed by a family, the more tension within that family. Professor Gerbner has argued that the values of heavy television viewers in regard to issues of premarital sex, extramarital sex, and violence differ sharply from those of light television viewers. Those who watch large amounts of television are more apt to live in fear of rape, murder, and the sundry crimes that come across their screens each evening than are those who watch fewer hours of television. When asked to estimate the crime rates, heavy television watchers select figures that are accurate in the electronic world but are far in excess of what we actually find in society. Some analysts call this "The Mean World Syndrome." Just as many have warned, people have begun to believe that the world of television is real and that their lives are the fantasy.

Television—not a true story

My major complaint against television is that most of the stories it tells simply are not true. A true story must either help us to see the world as it is or show what it can become. Most television stories do neither. On the one hand, as I have attempted to show, they create a fantasy world that breeds fear. On the other hand, television stories fail to create a new or better world or to offer a solution to the human dilemma. True stories lift our vision for the future or enable us to create a world that is more caring and humane.

Christians can never celebrate life as it is. In this world there is far too much suffering, injustice, and pain. In life as we now know it, the proud and greedy win too often, and the humble and generous succeed too infrequently. Not so in the world of the fable, folktale, or biblical story. Most of the classical stories demonstrate that the wages of sin is death. The greedy older brother loses his life on the Mountain of the Sun, the haughty sister is destroyed by her pride, and the traveler who ignores the crippled old woman standing in need by the side of the road never receives the magic key that helps open the door to the mysteries of life.

Classical stories do far more than to expose our failures; they also lift our spirits by pointing to our hope. The world of the folktale tells of an existence where justice is experienced, where truth reigns, and where the poor live happily ever after.

True stories carry and nurture us by helping us to see things as they are as well as what they can become. They invite us to identify with one of the characters or see ourselves in some aspect of the drama. Whether our response is aha! or ha, ha! (in some cases one is merely the flip side of the other), the true story has an impact on our lives, helping us understand our own stories.

How shall we deal with the mechanical storyteller that dominates life in so many American homes? The strategy of caring Christian families has varied, from severely limiting viewing time for children to totally eliminating television in the home.

Our suggestion is not just to stop listening to the false stories, which may be neither possible or desirable, but to begin telling the true stories again, stories that affirm honesty, fidelity, and generosity while exposing the deadliness of self-centered, greedy behavior. Our positive strategy is to again emphasize those stories that have informed and shaped previous generations. In a sense it is not only our privilege to do so, but our responsibility. For as Elie Wiesel has suggested, true stories are meant to be transmitted: "To keep them to oneself is to betray them."

Stories to live by

Richard Adam's novel *Watership Down* begins with the exodus of a small group of rabbits from a large, well-organized warren. Like the children of Israel, these rabbits are slaves who want a home of their own. With no specific geographical location in mind, they escape the clutches of The Threarah, a kind of rabbit pharaoh, and with a bit of luck, and even a miracle or two, set out for an unknown promised land.

Rabbits, Adams informs us early in the novel, are lovers of stories. Many of their stories tell of the adventures of El-ahrairah, the mischievous prince of rabbits.

Though the stories are clearly entertaining, their value goes far beyond simple enjoyment. Storytelling is the method these rabbits use to find their way through life. In the early days of their escape, the stories remind the travelers that they are a vulnerable species and must therefore live by wit, speed, and their strong sense of community. The stories help them remember their origins, tell them who they are and where they are going. In *Watership Down,* stories give the rabbits a sense of identity and help them survive.

Not long into their adventures, the exodus rabbits discover an unnamed warren where the residents have lost their sense of tradition. They no longer live by wit, speed, and ingenuity. There is no sense of community. Rather than teach the art of survival, the leaders of this warren teach the inevitability of death. Like people in our individualistic secular world, rabbits in this warren have no use for the traditional stories of the past. They believe that there is little value in the ancient myths, and certainly they are not so foolish as to believe in any mystical prince like El-ahrairah.

The exodus rabbits soon leave this liberal warren and continue their search for a new home. Their next contact is with Efrafa, a totalitarian rabbit community. Under the dictatorship of the giant rabbit, Woundwort, the animals in Efrafa are safe from predators and always well fed, as long as they perform the roles that are assigned to them. Like all totalitarian governments, Efrafa places a higher priority on security than on creative thought and human freedom.

Though Efrafa is quite different from the liberal warren, the two rabbit communities have at least one thing in common: neither remembers or believes in the stories of El-ahrairah. By ceasing to be a story people, both the liberal community and the totalitarian state cut themselves off from the finest traditions and values of the past.

In the end, the exodus rabbits defeat Woundwort and establish a warren on Watership Down. The key to their strategy, and ultimately their victory, comes from one of the stories of their prince, El-ahrairah. These sacred stories assist them in remembering the past and thus steering clear of the traps that other storyless rabbits fall into. Stories, Richard Adams suggests, help rabbits know who they are and where they are going.

Like the rabbits of *Watership Down,* we humans are storytelling creatures. Not only do we tell stories to entertain, but to learn from the past, to understand our world, and to grapple with the mysteries of life. Through stories we attempt to find patterns of significance in apparently meaningless events, as well as teach values to the next generation.

Unlike two of the rabbit communities, the problem we face today is not that people have stopped telling stories, but that they have stopped telling the traditional stories, the sacred stories that informed and shaped generations of our ancestors. The use of storytelling in ministry may be one way to counteract this problem.

2

STORYTELLING IN MINISTRY

The communication revolution brought about by the advent of television has not only changed the way we think and learn, it has dramatically altered our expectations of those who speak in public. Audiences, or, if you prefer, congregations, are no longer content to listen to someone read to them from a manuscript. They expect the speaker to make contact visually as well as intellectually. They prefer language that is vivid, concrete, and clear. People in the pew, along with the rest of the world, are much less tolerant of sloppy public address than folks from a generation ago. With the advent of TV, reading a sermon has been changed from a misdemeanor to a felony.

Television also allows people to choose, not only between their home pastor and the preacher down the road, but the smiling man from California who appears coast to coast in our living rooms each Sunday morning. Even pastors who don't like Robert Schuller's methods or theology must admit that he has mastered the 20th-century art of communication. He speaks without a note and in a manner that is clear and pictorial. Some people think of him as a storyteller.

Television, as we have seen, is a storytelling medium. Woe to those who do not understand the tool they use. Part of the reason for the success of Ronald Reagan is his superb use of television. The electronic evangelist who stands before the camera and reads a sermon from behind a pulpit is off the air faster than you can say Del Rio, Texas.

The reformers of the 16th century often referred to the church as a "mouth house." By this term they accented the importance of oral communication and the proclaimed Word. In a way, TV has brought us full circle. It demands that teachers and preachers develop oral skills to tell the story and proclaim the Word. Seen merely as an aid to public address, storytelling helps to energize delivery, improve eye contact, and make the message more concrete.

Storytelling, however, is an instrument of faith as well as communication. Just as our Lord used parables and stories to assist his disciples to envision the kingdom of God, so our stories can help people both see and hear what the gospel means. Amos Wilder suggested that the message and method of Jesus were inevitably tied together. It was impossible for Jesus to communicate his dynamic message through abstract language. If Wilder is correct, the use of storytelling is not simply a matter of taste, but an issue of faith. A message that is difficult to picture or envision in the mind's eye is nearly impossible to believe.

Andrew Greeley documented this concern in his sociological study of the "religious imagination" (faith) of Catholic young adults. He concluded, "The church seems to have overestimated the importance of propositional instruction and notably underestimated the importance of storytelling in the development of the religious imagination." Story evokes a more powerful faith response than doctrine and concept.

One of the major obstacles in the acceptance of storytelling in the church is that it is viewed as appropriate primarily for children. Many people believe that serious theology must be abstract.

Storytelling, they say, is something we use in Sunday schools, libraries, and children's sermons. Apparently some people do not realize that most of the Old Testament and the Gospels rely exclusively on story to communicate the word of God. Jesus was a storyteller.

Beldon Lane, in a 1981 article in *Christian Century,* suggested that we deal with this problem by adopting the Jewish distinction between *halakah* and *haggadah. Halakah* is reasoned reflection on the law and is primarily abstract in nature. In our tradition this includes most of the letters of Paul, the Catechism, and nearly all of current theology. *Halakah* is a necessary aspect of Christian reasoning; it assists us in thinking through complex problems about God and ethics.

Haggadah is the way of metaphor and picture. Ask a rabbi a question and you are likely to hear a story. Most of Jewish and Christian Scriptures are *haggadic* in nature. The Gospels are primarily stories about Jesus or stories that Jesus told. Some of the writings of Sören Kierkegaard, the Desert Fathers, and the *Table Talks* of Luther fall in this category.

A faithful church struggling with the mysteries of God and the challenge to proclaim the gospel to the world needs many ways to communicate. The primary method within the public assembly, I am convinced, will be *haggadah,* the way of story.

Reading the lessons

In too many congregations the reading of the lessons has become the most disappointing time during the entire liturgy. The use of bulletin inserts is our confession that our readers do not communicate effectively. All too often the Scripture is read with no emotion, eyes glued to the page. The congregation, insert in hand, follows unexpectantly, eyes also glued to the page. Where eyes never meet and passion is seldom expressed, a lot of effective communication is lost.

Part of the reason that listening to the lessons can be so dreadful is that few readers prepare orally. At a clergy conference only two of 55 pastors present indicated they practiced reading the Gospel out loud before the service began. Most of those present indicated they read it once or twice silently in their studies. Good reading requires both skill and practice.

An increasing number of pastors and lay people are committing the lessons and Gospels to memory in order to free them from the page and allow a more powerful presentation. A lay person thanked me for encouraging her pastor to use the discipline of memorizing each Sunday's Gospel by saying, "Listening to the Gospel has become a high point in worship for the entire congregation."

Whenever the Lesson is in story form, it invites us to tell rather than read it. Better oral presentations help the Word sound fresh and alive to the listener.

Teaching

Some teachers in our church schools spend more time preparing the craft material than the Bible story. It is sad when our children take home a burned match cross or some other cute item but fail to remember what the lesson was about that day.

One of the most powerful ways of presenting the Bible story is simply to *tell* it, with nothing—not even a book—coming between the teacher and student. I encourage teachers to tell the story at least twice during each session. Often a second, or even a third, telling allows the children to join in the story much like they do when a favorite book is reread.

One of my goals in teaching my junior high class is to have the students not only hear and know the stories of God, but to learn to tell them. Class time is spent primarily listening and telling Bible stories. I am more concerned that they know the story than that they are able to say what I—the teacher—think it means. If they know and remember the story, I trust that one day they will be able to use it as a resource for their lives.

Though biblical stories are the prime resource for the Christian teacher, traditional folktales and fables are also valuable. Some folktales, like "The Grain of Rice" found in Chapter 5, can be told immediately after a parable. The listeners can then discover the meaning of the parable by exploring both the differences and similarities of the two stories.

Most often, however, the folktale is used in Christian education because it reinforces the teaching of the biblical story or says something similar in an unexpected way. One of the difficulties with reading Scripture is that we know it so well that it no longer surprises or shocks us. The use of an appropriate fable or folktale can actually help us get in touch with the Word.

Folktales

What attracts me to the world of the folktale is the sense of moral urgency that rings from nearly every story. All folktales seem to cry out, "What you do is of ultimate importance!" In the world of the folktale, even what appears to be an insignificant choice often has near-cosmic consequences. Life in this arena, C. K. Chesterton has written, hangs by a thread. The king may invite fairies to the christening, but he must invite all the fairies or frightful results will follow. A promise is broken to a cat and the whole world goes wrong. A girl is given a box on condition she does not open it; she opens it, and all kinds of evil rush out. This ought to sound familiar to Christians who tell a story about a man and woman who are put in a garden with the simple condition that they avoid eating the fruit from a single tree. They eat it, and their world is never the same again. In fact, our world is never the same.

Folktales warn us of the dire consequences of breaking our promises or of being greedy, hoarding people. Pride is not just inconvenient, it is destructive. It is imperative that we become what we are meant to be.

Some critics play down the value of folk literature by pointing to the excessive violence in some tales and the banality in others. Of course, folktales, like other forms of literature, are uneven. Few people would dismiss the value of all novels just because some are of inferior quality. The same is true in Scripture. Who would claim that the Book of Esther is on the same plane as Genesis or that the Letter of Jude is as profound as Paul's epistle to the Romans? When I claim that folktales can enrich our lives, I mean that certain folktales are valuable.

In this collection I have leaned heavily on Jewish and German stories. To identify any story with a particular country is a bit unfair, for the reader of folktales soon discovers that many of the best stories are found in the collections of more than one country. Experts explain that travelers passed on their best stories to people in other cultures, who adapted them by changing the names and a few of the events. Still, stories are often identified with a single country, and some, particularly Jewish stories, have a unique character. Jewish stories are the most usable for our purposes because they share a common understanding of God and because they are teaching stories.

Although Jewish people told stories for entertainment, there is virtually not a single story that does not assume the existence of one God or does not teach a moral lesson. Many of these stories, like the parables of Jesus, change the way the listener sees the world.

Fables

Although the fables of Aesop were long thought to be the work of a single Greek slave who lived five centuries before the birth of Christ, most scholars today believe Aesop was an early collector, much like the brothers Grimm in Germany.

Like all folk literature, fables have been revised by each culture that has touched and used them. Fables as they now exist were probably compiled in the late medieval period and almost certainly bear the imprint of Christian monks.

Martin Luther studied fables as a schoolboy and thought that every student ought to have the opportunity to encounter the wisdom of these stories. He was amazed that such a book could be written so concisely and simply. "There is assuredly in Aesop more instruction than in the whole of Jerome," he once declared in his *Table Talks*. Later, Luther wrote, "After the Bible, the writings of Cato and Aesop are the best; better than all the opinions of the philosophers and jurists." For Luther, Aesop was the chief book of worldly wisdom, while the Bible was the chief book of spiritual wisdom.

Though Luther used fables in his preaching and teaching, he was not fond of moralizing. One commentator put it this way, "He used fables in his preaching but he would do no preaching in his fables." His advice to us might well have been, "Just tell the story and let the listener figure it out." Altogether too many preachers and speakers insult the intelligence of their listeners by telling a story and then promptly draining it of all meaning by a lengthy analysis.

Luther found time to translate 20 of these fables, and he intended to translate and publish all the existing fables of Aesop. Unfortunately it was a work that was never completed. Other Reformation writers also loved fables and often used them as vehicles of satire and protest in their verbal fight with Rome.

Isaac Singer has written that the fable is particularly enjoyable in the 1980s, a time of literary verbosity, when writers often invest more words in analysis and interpretation than in telling the story. This ancient literary form is both concise and direct.

Fables teach morality and wisdom primarily by their vivid portraits of character. The focus of a fable is not so much on good works as on bad. They act as law, not gospel, exposing the folly and stupidity of human beings. In these stories greed, envy, anger, and stupidity lead people down a road where judgment is swift and sure. Fables fit our definition of a true story because even though they do not tell us what the world can become, they show us the world as it is by exposing our human foibles and weaknesses.

The fable appears to be from the same genre as the proverb. Many of them are extended proverbs, or at least proverbs in story form. Even the issues addressed by biblical proverbs and the stories of Aesop are similar. The wise person must eschew flattery and pompous behavior and cultivate honesty and virtue. Vain and greedy people end up suffering the consequences of their own foolish activity.

By the almost exclusive use of animals, fables focus on the universal characteristics of life rather than on specific individuals. Quickly the listener understands that the issue is not so much the stupidity of a particular character as a whole class of people. Upon finishing the fable, one concludes, "My pride is self-defeating and my greed leads toward death." In fables characters are most predictable. The fox is always cunning, the hare timid, the lion bold, the wolf cruel, the bull strong, and the ass patient.

Many writers have tried their hand at crafting fables. Some have found the precision of the fable a difficult format to master. In addition to fables out of Aesop's collection, works adapted from Leo Tolstoy, Ivan Kriloff, Jonathan Swift, Christian Gellert, Gotthold Lessing, John Aikin, and La Fontaine are included in this volume.

3

STORIES OF LOVE AND COMPASSION

God is Good

The goodness and love of God is evident to the eyes of faith during bad times as well as good, as this Jewish folktale shows.

Two men set out on a journey together. They took a donkey to carry their packs, a torch to light their way at night, and a rooster, who was a friend of the donkey. The rooster sat on the donkey's head during the entire journey.

One of the men was deeply religious; the second was a skeptic. On the journey they frequently spoke about the Lord. "In all things, God is good," said the first companion.

"We will see if your opinion bears out on the trip," said the second.

Shortly before dusk the two men arrived in a small village where they sought a place to sleep. Despite their frequent requests, no one offered them a night's lodging. Reluctantly, they traveled a mile outside of town, where they decided to sleep.

"I thought you said God is good," the skeptic said sarcastically.

"God has decided this is the best place for us to sleep tonight," replied his friend.

They fixed their beds beneath a large tree, just off the main road that led to the village, tethering the donkey about 30 yards away. Just as they were about to light the torch they heard a horrible noise. A lion had killed the donkey and carried it off to eat it away from the two men. Quickly the companions climbed the tree to stay away from danger.

"You still say God is good?" the skeptic asked with anger.

"If the lion hadn't eaten the donkey, he would have attacked us. God is good," his companion declared.

Moments later a cry from the rooster sent them further up the tree. From this new vantage point they saw a wildcat carrying the cock away in his teeth.

Before the skeptic could say a word, the man of faith declared, "The cry of the rooster has once again saved us. God is good."

A few minutes later a strong wind arose and blew out the torch, the only comfort of the men in the black night. Again the skeptic taunted his companion. "It appears that the goodness of God is working overtime this evening," he said. This time the believer was silent.

The next morning the two men walked back into the village for food. They soon discovered that a large band of outlaws had swept into town the previous night and robbed the entire village of all its possessions.

With this news the man of faith turned to his friend. "Finally it has become clear," he cried. "Had we been given a room in the village last night, we would have been robbed along with all of the villagers. If the wind had not blown out our torch, the bandits who traveled the road near the place where we slept would have discovered us and taken all our goods. It is clear, that in all things, God is good."

What You Have Done for the Least

This story has been adapted from a tale by Leo Tolstoy. Although there are many other stories about encountering Christ as we care for people in need, few match the simplicity and power of the Tolstoy version.

Many years ago there was a shoemaker named Martin who lived in a tiny cellar apartment in a large city in Russia. The only light in his room came from a small window, just high enough to see people walking by from the knee down. Martin was a busy shoemaker, for he was an honest man and a fine craftsman.

Martin lived alone. His wife had died while he was still an apprentice, leaving him with one son. The boy died 10 years later, at age 13, leaving his father lonely and depressed.

In his trouble the shoemaker had sought the counsel of a holy man. "All I ask of God is that he bring my life quickly to a close," Martin told him. "I have become a man without hope."

"There is still reason for you to live," said the old man. "The answer lies in God. When you give yourself to God you will find the reason to live, and you will no longer grieve over your great loss."

Martin pondered the man's words. "How do I give myself to God?" he finally asked.

"That is what Christ showed us. Purchase and read the New Testament. There you will learn to live for God. Everything is to be found in the Gospels."

Deeply moved, Martin went immediately to a store where he bought a New Testament. Each night, after his work was finished, Martin lit his lamp and read from the precious book. The more he read, the more he understood. The more he understood, the clearer and more joyful his heart became.

As the depression left him, Martin faced each day with great anticipation. He worked long hours, caring tenderly for the boots and shoes that entered his tiny shop. His night reading empowered him to do his finest work.

One night Martin was reading the seventh chapter of St. Luke's gospel. The story was about a rich Pharisee who invited the Lord to his house as a guest. While Jesus sat at the table, a sinful woman anointed his feet and bathed him with her tears. In the end Jesus absolved the woman of all her sin.

Martin put the book down and closed his eyes. He could imagine what controversy that incident had caused.

Opening his eyes he looked again at the story. "Then turning toward the woman [Jesus] said to Simon, 'Do you see this woman? I entered your house, you gave me no water for my feet, but she has wet my feet with her tears and wiped them with her hair. You gave me no kiss, but from the time I came in, she has not ceased to kiss my feet. You did not anoint my head with oil, but she has anointed my feet with ointment" (Luke 7:44-46).

Again Martin closed his eyes "Would I have been like the Pharisee?" he wondered. "He took care of himself but ignored his guest. And the guest was the Lord himself! If he came to me, would I have done the same?"

In a moment Martin fell asleep, still sitting in his chair.

"Martin!" A voice seemed to breathe in his ear.

Martin roused himself, half-awake. "Who is there?" he mumbled.

"Martin, look out in the street tomorrow. I will come to visit you!"

Suddenly Martin was fully awake. Was this the voice of Christ? Had he only imagined the words? Uncertain, he sat and paced for nearly an hour before he blew out the lamp and went to bed again.

The next morning Martin rose before dawn, prayed, heated the stove, put on his cabbage soup, and sat down at his bench by the window to work. This morning, however, his mind was not on shoes. He wondered about the voice that he heard, or thought he heard, the night before. Though one part of him suggested that the whole incident was just a dream, another part desperately wanted the Lord to visit.

Like a schoolboy, Martin's eyes wandered out the window most of the morning. He saw familiar boots pass by in the new snow. As he stared he could see old Stephen, the retired soldier who served as an assistant janitor in the building, come out to clear away the snow. From the beginning the old man struggled.

"He is worn out already," Martin thought when he saw Stephen lean on his shovel against the wall. "A man that old and frail has no business shoveling the heavy snow." Tapping on the window, he cried out to the old man, "Come in and get warm. I have some tea ready."

Moments later old Stephen shuffled into the small room. "Christ keep you, my bones are aching."

"Don't bother wiping your feet," Martin advised. "I have to mop soon anyway." He poured two glasses of tea and offered one, with a sugar cube, to his visitor. Without speaking the old man drank down the glass, turned it bottom up, sucked what remained of the tea through the cube, and nodded his thanks to his host.

"Have another," Martin said, reaching for the teapot.

Stephen drank this also, though not quite so quickly. As the old soldier drank, Martin glanced out the window.

"Are you waiting for someone?" Stephen asked.

"Waiting? Well, yes I am, though I am rather embarrassed about it." He then told the old man of his dream. "It all began when I was reading about Jesus at the house of the Pharisee. Have you heard of the story?"

"Heard of it, yes, but I can't read."

Martin told him the entire tale, and when he showed interest, told him other stories as well. When he finished, both men were silent. Finally Martin asked, "More tea?"

"I have had enough," Stephen said, rising. "Thank you for inviting me; you have fed both my body and my soul."

Martin was pleased as the old man went outside, but he was also a bit disappointed. It was already late morning, and Jesus had not yet come. He moved back to the workbench. He watched as other shoes passed by his window. He paced the floor impatiently.

On one of his trips to the door he saw a woman, poorly dressed, standing against the wall with her back to the wind. She had a child in her arms. She wore summer clothes and the blanket around the baby was thin and ragged.

Opening the door, Martin cried out, "My good woman, it is easier to wrap the baby in here where it is warm."

In a moment the woman was standing by the stove telling her story. Her husband had gone off to war eight months before and hadn't been heard from since. She had worked as a cook until the baby was born four months ago. "They laid me off," she said sadly.

"Don't you have any warm clothes?"

"I sold my last shawl yesterday for 20 coins. We needed the food."

"Come," Martin said. He took her to his tiny closet where a woman's winter coat was hanging. "It belonged to my wife. I don't need it anymore." Before she left he gave her a bowl of the cabbage soup and found a warm blanket for the baby.

When she was gone Martin felt pleased that he had been able to assist her in some small way. He also felt sad, for it was early afternoon, and Jesus had not yet made his visit.

As the afternoon wore on, he found it difficult to keep his mind on his work. He often peered into the street through his tiny window and opened his door. As he was standing in the door midway though the afternoon, he saw an old woman carrying a basket of apples on one arm and a sack of wood chips for her fire on the other. As she stopped outside Martin's door to shift the basket, a small boy snatched an apple out of the basket and began to run away. The old woman grabbed him by the sleeve and held on. The boy struggled to get loose, but the determined woman would not let go. Martin jumped up and ran outside without taking time to put on his coat. When he reached the pair the woman was pulling the boy's hair and he was screaming.

Martin separated the two, and taking the boy by the hand, he pleaded, "Let him go, grandmother. Forgive and forget, for the sake of Christ."

"I'll give him something he won't forget," she shouted. "I'll take him to the police."

"For the sake of Christ," Martin pleaded, "have mercy."

In the next few moments a beautiful drama was enacted. The old woman released the boy. He apologized. After Martin talked to her about the forgiveness of the Savior, she gave the lad another apple and smiled. As she took her basket and headed home the boy sprang forward and offered to carry the sack of wood chips. Martin moved to the door and watched the two walk down the street together.

As he went back inside he felt good that he had been able to help the two settle their differences. He also felt sad because it was now late afternoon, and Jesus had not come.

The shoemaker put his tools away, swept the floor, and set his table. When he finished the last of the cabbage soup, Martin picked up the New Testament and sat in his chair by the lamp. He felt rather foolish for believing that Jesus had spoken to him the night before.

He opened the sacred book to the 25th chapter of St. Matthew. There he read, "Then the righteous will answer him, 'Lord, when did we see thee hungry and feed thee, or thirsty and give thee drink? And when did we see thee a stranger, and welcome thee, or naked and clothe thee? And when did we see thee sick or in prison and visit thee?' And the king will answer them, 'Truly, I say to you, as you did it to one of the least of these my brethren, you did it to me.' "

Images of old Stephen and the soldier's wife and the woman and the boy suddenly flashed across his mind. Then Martin realized that his dream had not deceived him; the Savior had truly come to him that day, and he had truly received him.

The Two Brothers

There is a surprising quality to love, be it the love of God or that of his people. This Jewish folktale links the surprise to an old Temple legend.

There were once two brothers who farmed together. They shared equally in all of the work and split the profits exactly. Each had his own granary. One of the brothers was married and had a large family; the other brother was single.

One day the single brother thought to himself, "It is not fair that we divide the grain evenly. My brother has many mouths to feed, while I have but one. I know what I'll do, I will take a sack of grain from my granary each evening and put it in my brother's granary." So, each night when it was dark, he carefully carried a sack of grain, placing it in his brother's barn.

Now the married brother thought to himself, "It is not fair that we divide the grain evenly. I have many children to care for me in my old age, and my brother has none. I know what I'll do, I will take a sack of grain from my granary each evening and put it in my brother's granary." And he did.

Each morning the two brothers were amazed to discover that though they had removed a sack of grain the night before, they had just as many.

One night the two brothers met each other halfway between their barns, each carrying a sack of grain. Then they understood the mystery. And they embraced, and loved each other deeply.

There is a legend that says God looked down from heaven, saw the two brothers embracing, and said, "I declare this to be a holy place, for I have witnessed extraordinary love here." It is also said that it was on that spot that Solomon built the first temple.

The Happy Prince

This is an adaption of a story by the 19th-century writer, Oscar Wilde.

High above the city, on a tall column, stood the statue of the Happy Prince. He was gilded all over with thin leaves of fine gold, for eyes he had two bright sapphires, and a large red ruby glowed in his sword-hilt.

He was very much admired. The Town Councilors thought the Happy Prince brought honor to their city, and the small children said that he looked just like an angel, though none of them had ever seen an angel. Parents pointed to the Happy Prince with pride and urged their children to be content and peaceful like the beautiful statue.

One night there flew over the city a little Swallow. His friends had gone away to Egypt six weeks before, but he had been delayed.

When he arrived in the city he immediately began to search for a proper place to stay. When he spotted the statue on the tall column he decided to sleep between the feet of the Happy Prince.

Just as he prepared to go to sleep by putting his head under his wing, a large drop of water fell on him. "What a curious thing," he cried. "There is not a single cloud in the sky, the stars are quite clear and bright, and yet it is raining. The climate in the north of Europe is really dreadful."

Then another drop fell. And a third.

Just as the Swallow decided to move to a dryer location, he looked up to see tears running down the golden cheeks of the Happy Prince. His face was so beautiful in the moonlight that the little Swallow was filled with pity.

"Who are you?" he said.

"I am the Happy Prince."

"Why are you weeping then?" asked the Swallow.

"When I was alive and had a human heart," answered the statue, "I did not know what tears were, for I lived in the Palace of Sans-Souci, where sorrow is not allowed to enter. In the daytime I played with my companions in the garden, and in the evening I led the dance in the Great Hall. Round the garden ran a very lofty wall, but I never cared to ask what lay beyond it, everything about me was so beautiful. My courtiers called me the Happy Prince, and happy indeed I was, if pleasure be happiness. So I lived, and so I died. And now that I am dead they have set me up here so high that I can see all the ugliness and the misery of my city, and though my heart is made of lead yet I cannot choose but weep."

"What! Is he not solid gold?" the Swallow thought. He was too polite to make any personal remarks out loud.

"Far away," continued the statue in a low musical voice, "far away in a little street there is a poor house. One of the windows is open, and through it I can see a woman seated at a table. Her face is thin and worn, and she has coarse, red hands, all pricked by the needle, for she is a seamstress.

"In a bed in the corner of the room her little boy is lying ill. He has a fever and is asking for oranges. His mother has nothing to give him but river water, so he is crying. Swallow, Swallow, little Swallow, will you not bring her the ruby out of my sword-hilt? My feet are fastened to this pedestal and I cannot move."

"My friends are waiting for me in Egypt," said the Swallow. "At present they are flying up and down the Nile, but soon they will go to sleep in the tomb of the great King. The King is wrapped in yellow linen, lying in his coffin, enbalmed with spices."

"Swallow, Swallow, little Swallow," said the Prince, "will you not stay with me for one night, and be my messenger? The boy is so thirsty. and the mother is so sad."

"I don't think I like boys," answered the Swallow. "Last summer the miller's two rude sons threw stones at me. Of course they never hit me, swallows fly far too well for that, but still it was a mark of disrespect." ·

But the Happy Prince looked so sad that the little swallow was sorry. "It is very cold here, but I will stay with you for one night and be your messenger," he said.

"Thank you, little Swallow," said the Prince.

So the Swallow picked out the great ruby from the Prince's sword and flew away with it in his beak over the roofs of the town. He passed over the cathedral tower, where the white marble angels were sculptured. He passed by the palace and heard the sound of dancing. He passed over the river and saw the lanterns hanging to the masts of the ships.

At last he came to a poor house and looked in. The boy was tossing feverishly on his bed, and the mother had fallen asleep. In he hopped, and he laid the great ruby on the table beside the woman's thimble. Then he flew gently round the bed, fanning the boys's forehead with his wings. "How cool I feel," murmured the boy. "I must be getting better." Then he sank into a delicious slumber.

Then the Swallow flew back to the Happy Prince and told him what he had done. "It is curious," he remarked, "but I feel quite warm now, although it is so cold."

"That is because you have done a good action," said the Prince. And the little Swallow began to think, and then he fell asleep.

When day broke the Swallow flew down to the river and had a bath. People were surprised to see a Swallow in winter. He flew all about the town for one last look before he headed south to Egypt.

When the moon rose he flew back to the Happy Prince. "Have you any commissions for Egypt?" he cried. "I am just starting."

"Swallow, Swallow, little Swallow," said the Prince, "will you not stay with me one night longer?"

"My friends wait for me in Egypt," protested the Swallow.

"Far away across the city I see a young man in a tiny attic apartment. He is leaning over a desk covered with papers, and in a tumbler by his side there is a bunch of withered violets. His hair is brown and crisp, and his lips are red as a pomegranate. He is trying to finish a play for the director of the theater, but he is too cold to write any more. There is no fire in the grate, and hunger has made him faint."

"I will wait with you one night longer," said the Swallow, who really had a good heart. "Shall I take another ruby?"

"Alas! I have no ruby now," said the Prince. "My eyes are all that I have left. They are made of rare sapphires which were brought out of India a thousand years ago. Pluck out one of them and take it to him. He will sell it to the jeweler and buy firewood and finish his play."

"Dear Prince," said the Swallow, "I cannot do that." And he began to weep.

"Swallow, Swallow, little Swallow," said the Prince, "do as I command you."

So the Swallow plucked out the Prince's eye and flew away to the student's apartment. It was easy enough to get in, as there was a hole in the roof. Through this he darted and came into the room. The young man had his head buried in his hands, so he did not hear the flutter of the bird's wings, and when he looked up he found the beautiful sapphire lying on the withered violets.

"This is a gift from a great admirer," cried the student. "Now I can finish my play."

The next day the Swallow flew down to the harbor. He sat on the mast of a large vessel and shouted, "I am going to Egypt." No one seemed to notice, and when the moon was full he flew back to the Happy Prince.

"I have come to bid you good-bye," he cried.

"Swallow, Swallow, little Swallow," said the Prince, "will you not stay with me one night longer?"

"It is winter," answered the Swallow, "and the snow will soon be here. In Egypt the sun is warm, and my companions are building a nest in the Temple of Baalbek. I must leave you now, but I will never forget you, and next spring I will bring you back two beautiful jewels in place of those you have given away. The ruby shall be redder than a red rose, and the sapphire shall be as blue as the great sea."

"In the square below," said the Happy Prince, "there stands a little match-girl. She has let her matches fall in the gutter, and they are all spoiled. Her father will beat her if she does not bring home some money, and she is crying. She has not shoes or stockings, and her little head is bare. Pluck out my other eye and give it to her, and her father will not beat her."

"I will stay with you one night longer," said the Swallow, "but I cannot pluck out your eye. You would be quite blind then."

"Swallow, Swallow, little Swallow," said the Prince, "do as I command you."

So he plucked out the Prince's other eye and darted down with it. He swooped past the match-girl and slipped the jewel into the palm of her hand. "What a lovely bit of glass!" cried the little girl, and she ran home laughing.

Then the Swallow came back to the Prince. "You are blind now," he said, "so I will stay with you always."

"No, little Swallow," said the poor Prince, "you must go away to Egypt."

"I will stay with you always," said the Swallow, and he slept at the Prince's feet.

All the next day he sat on the Prince's shoulder, and told him stories of what he had seen in strange lands. He told him of the Sphinx, who is as old as the world itself, and of the merchants who walk slowly by the side of their camels carrying amber beads in their hands. He told him of green snakes and red ibises and gold fish.

"Dear little Swallow," said the Prince, "you tell me of marvelous things, but more marvelous than anything is the suffering of men and women. Fly over my city, little Swallow, and tell me what you see there."

So the Swallow flew over the great city and saw beggars sitting at the gates of palaces and starving children looking listlessly at the black streets. Then he flew back and told the Prince what he had seen.

"I am covered with fine gold," said the prince. "You must take it off, leaf by leaf, and give it to my poor. The living always think that gold can make them happy."

Leaf after leaf of the fine gold the Swallow picked off, till the Happy Prince looked quite dull and grey. Leaf after leaf of the fine gold he brought to the poor, and the children's faces grew rosier, and they laughed and played games in the street. "We have bread now!" they cried.

Then the snow came, and after the snow came the frost. The streets were so bright and glistening that they looked as if they were made of silver. Long icicles like crystal daggers hung down from the eaves of the houses, everybody went about in furs, and the little boys wore scarlet caps and skated on the ice.

The poor little Swallow grew colder and colder, but he would not leave the Prince he loved so well. He picked up crumbs outside the baker's door and tried to keep himself warm by flapping his wings.

But at last he knew that he was going to die. He had just enough strength to fly up to the Prince's shoulder once more. "Good-bye, dear prince!" he murmured. "Will you let me kiss your hand?"

"I am glad that you are going to Egypt at last, little Swallow," said the Prince. "You have stayed too long here, but you must kiss me on the lips, for I love you."

"It is not to Egypt I am going," said the Swallow. "I am going to the House of Death. Death is the brother of Sleep, is he not?"

And he kissed the Happy Prince on the lips and fell down dead at his feet.

At that moment a curious crack sounded inside the statue, as if something had broken. The fact is that the leaden heart had snapped right in two.

Early the next morning the Mayor and the Town Councilors were walking in the town square. As they passed the column they looked up at the statue. "Dear me, how shabby the Happy Prince looks," the Mayor said. "The ruby has fallen out of the sword, his eyes are gone, and he is no longer golden. He looks little better than a beggar."

"Little better than a beggar," the Town Councilors agreed.

"And there is a dead bird at his feet," the Mayor continued. "It is disgusting."

The Town Councilors pulled down the statue of the Happy Prince and ordered it to be melted down at the foundry. Several days later the foreman at the foundry reported that though the furnace was very hot it was not able to melt the broken lead heart. "We must throw it away," he said. So they threw it on a dustheap where the dead Swallow was also lying.

"Bring me the two most precious things in the city," said God to one of his angels. The angel brought him the leaden heart and the dead bird.

"You have rightly chosen," said God, "for in my garden of paradise this little bird shall sing forevermore, and in my city of gold the Happy Prince shall praise me."

Victor

The inspiration for this story comes from Augustus, *a story by Herman Hesse. It reminds us that the essentials of life such as meaning, pleasure, and love ought not be sought directly. Rather, in the words of the prayer of St. Francis, it is in giving that we receive, it is in pardoning that we are pardoned, and, as Victor discovers, it is in loving that we are loved.*

Not very many years ago a young woman gave birth to her first child just one month after her husband died in a tragic accident. The neighbors, deeply concerned over the plight of the poor young widow, held a shower for the baby. Each person brought a beautiful present to help the mother and child get started in life.

Mrs. Binz, who lived directly across the street, brought a small crib. "All three of my children slept in that very bed," she said proudly.

"I have managed to find all these baby clothes on sale," the neighbor to the south explained, opening the presents herself.

Some of the friends brought meat, potatoes, or other foods. When all of the gifts were opened, the mother wept. "Thank you for your wonderful support," she said, brushing back the tears. "You have made a most difficult time much easier." She paused before she concluded, "Next Sunday my son will be baptized. I have decided to name him Victor after his father."

When all of the guests had left, the young widow heard a knock on the door. She opened it to find an old man who lived in the corner house by himself. Everyone called him Doc Burns, though he wasn't a doctor in any normal sense. Few people had ever talked to the reclusive old man, though he often waved at the widow as she walked past his home.

"I have come to give you my gift for your young son," he said softly. "Mine is a different kind of gift than the others you have received. I have come to offer you one wish for young Victor. It may be anything that you want. You must make the wish before the child is baptized on Sunday." He paused a moment and then continued, "Please believe that I have the power to give you whatever you desire for your beautiful son." Having concluded, the little man bowed and walked back to his house on the corner.

The young mother was baffled by the words of her strange little friend. Did he really have the power to grant a wish? What should she ask for? All week long she could not make up her mind. Finally, as they walked forward to the baptismal font, she whispered in the infant's ear, "I wish that everyone in the world will love my Victor."

And the wish came true. Victor grew up to be a handsome lad with jet black hair and gleaming white teeth. As a toddler, people could not resist hugging and touching him. Even when he was naughty, no one could believe that he had done anything wrong.

As he grew older Victor became known and loved throughout the village. He was always given food and toys by other children. If his mother scolded or punished him, the adults would insist that she was being too harsh to such a wonderful child. Victor responded to all this attention by treating people with scorn and contempt. Still they seemed to adore him.

As the years passed, even when Victor had trouble at home, he maintained a deep respect for Doc Burns. He often visited the old man and listened to his advice carefully. Doc was the only person who could reprimand Victor without the boy becoming angry or sullen.

When Victor graduated from high school, he was given a scholarship to a college in the east. At Christmas, when he returned home for the first time, he drove up in a beautiful, black Cadillac. His trunks were filled with fine clothes, and he had plenty of spending money. He seldom saw his mother during the vacation. He spent his nights out drinking at parties and taverns.

After college, Victor never worked but continued to live a life of ease. "I collect horses, dogs, and women," he often bragged. There was no pleasure he did not indulge in, and there was no vice he did not practice. No relationship was permanent. Even though women smothered him with attention and friends raved about him, his heart grew empty and his soul sick. He despised people who catered to him. He was disgusted with everything and everyone.

One night Victor decided to commit suicide. He withdrew to his bedroom where he mixed a powerful poison in a glass of wine and lifted it to his lips. Just as he was about to drink it, Doc Burns rushed through the door and took the glass out of his hands. "Good evening, Victor. It has been a long time since we have had a chance to talk," the old man said softly.

Ignoring Victor's plea to leave him alone, Doc Burns began to speak. "You seem to be satiated with your life of frivolity. I am sorry it has been such a meaningless existence for you. I suppose I am the one responsible for your misery. I fulfilled your mother's wish on the day of your Baptism, even though it was a foolish one. Suppose I now offer you a new wish? Make it anything you want, and I will fulfill it. Be careful, Victor," the old man concluded. "Wishes have a way of coming true."

"I don't think you can give me anything that I haven't already had," Victor said sadly.

"Think again, my son," Doc Burns said earnestly. "What has given you true happiness in your short life? Make another wish for my sake, and for the sake of your dear mother."

Victor closed his eyes and thought for several minutes. Finally he spoke through his tears, "Take away the old magic and give me a new wish. Rather than being loved, I ask for the ability to love everyone in the world."

"That was good," Doc Burns said, embracing the sobbing young man. "Now things will go better for you."

Things did go better for Victor, but not immediately. Without his great charm, he began to be abandoned by his friends. Several people retaliated for the past wrongs he had inflicted on them. He was thrown into jail for three months, and no one came to visit him. When he was released, he was sick, lonely, and penniless.

He returned home to nurse his ailing mother. For the first time in his life he was able to return her great love.

After his mother's recovery, Victor took a job as a janitor in an elementary school. He not only cared for clean floors, but for the children, particularly those who came from poor homes. To all the children he became "Mr. Victor," their friend and companion.

Finally he met a beautiful young widow who had two small children. They married, and he gave all three of them the love that they so desperately needed.

Poor in money, Victor was one of the richest men in the world. He discovered that it is in loving, not being loved, that life comes to its fullest expression.

The Little Dog

This story is adapted from a fable by John Aikin, an English writer.

One day a little puppy took a walk around his master's farm. When he came to the pen where the horse was fed he heard the great animal call to him. "You must be new here," the horse cried. "You will soon find out that the master loves me more than all other animals because I carry large loads for him. I suspect that an animal of your size is of no value to him at all."

The little dog hung his head and was about to walk away when he heard the cow in an adjoining stall. "*I* have the most honored position on the farm because the lady makes butter and cheese from my milk. You, of course, provide nothing of value to the family."

"Cow, your position is no greater than mine," called the sheep. "I lend the master wool to make his clothes. I provide warmth to the entire family. You are correct, however, about the dog," the sheep concluded. "He gives the master nothing."

One by one the animals joined in the conversation, telling about their honored positions on the farm. The chicken told how she produced eggs, and the cat, famous for her quickness, how she rid the house of mice. All the animals did agree on one thing: the little dog provided no service of value to the farm family.

Stung by the criticism of the other animals, the puppy found a secluded place away from the animals and began to cry. An old dog heard the sobs and paused to listen to the little one tell his story. "They are right," he sobbed. "I provide no service to anyone."

"It is true," the old dog began, "that you are too small to pull the wagon. And you will never produce eggs, milk, or wool. But it is foolish to cry about what you cannot do. You must use the ability the Creator gave you to bring laughter and cheer."

That night, when the master came home exhausted from long hours in the hot sun, the little puppy ran to him, licked his feet and jumped into his arms. Falling to the ground, the master and puppy romped in the grass. Finally, holding him close to his chest and patting his head, the master said, "No matter how tired I am when I get home, I feel better when you greet me. I wouldn't trade you for all the animals on the farm."

"*. . . and the greatest of these is love.*"

Magic Mustard Seeds

The answer to sorrow, as well as loneliness, often lies in our willingness and ability to enter into the lives of others and share in their pain, as this Jewish folktale says so powerfully.

Once a widow's son died in a tragic accident. The woman, crazy with grief, mourned her loss so deeply that no one could provide her with comfort. At last a friend took her to the house of a holy man where she made a sobbing plea. "Use your powers to bring my son back to life. Surely you are able by prayer or some magic to induce the Almighty to lighten my grief."

The old man spoke kindly to the woman, "Bring me a mustard seed from a home that has never known sorrow. I will use that seed to remove the pain from your life."

Immediately the woman set out in search of the magic mustard seed. "First I will visit the home of a wealthy family," she thought. "Tragedy is less likely to strike them." Soon she approached a beautiful mansion, knocked on the door, and spoke to the woman who greeted her. "I am in search of a home that has never known sorrow. Is this such a place? Please, it is vital that I know."

"Never known sorrow!" cried the woman who had answered the door. "You have come to the wrong house." As she sobbed she began to describe all of the tragedies that had touched her family. She invited the widow into her home to explain in greater detail what had taken place. The widow remained in that home for many days, listening and caring.

When she left to resume her search the widow visited a modest home about a mile away. The experience was the same. Wherever she traveled, from mansion to hut, she was greeted with tales of sadness and sorrow. Everyone found her a willing and careful listener.

After months of travel she became so involved with the grief of others that she forgot about her search for the magic mustard seed, never realizing that it had indeed driven the sorrow from her life.

4

STORIES OF SAINTS AND SINNERS

The Legend of Babouschka

Many years ago a woman whose name was Babouschka lived alone in a cold, barren, and lonely part of Russia. Though her home was tiny, really nothing more than a hut, she worked hard each day keeping it very clean. There was little else for Babouschka to do since she did not see people for days at a time, even though her house was on a corner where four roads met.

One night, in the coldest time of winter, when Babouschka had finished eating her meal, she suddenly heard the sounds of men and animals off in the distance. Moving quickly to her window, she saw a great procession inching its way toward her house. When they reached her door, they stopped. Babouschka had never seen such a group before. Three kings wearing magnificent crowns led the group. They rode camels, and a host of servants walked at their sides. As Babouschka peered through her curtain she heard one of the kings address his servants.

"Go to the house and see if the people who live there can give us directions."

Obediently, the servants approached and rapped on the door. Babouschka was frightened and refused to answer. After several minutes the servant returned to his master and gestured in the direction of the hut. After deliberating for a few minutes, all three kings got off their camels and approached the door.

"Please," one of them shouted, "open the door and give us directions. We mean you no harm."

Babouschka moved cautiously to the door and opened it carefully. "Who are you?" she cried.

"We are men who study the stars. We have seen a sign, that a young child is to be born who brings a great message from God. He will be King of kings and Lord of lords. We bring him our finest gifts and wish to offer him our allegiance."

Babouschka could see precious gifts hanging from the camels. "I am a stupid old woman who has never traveled more than four hours beyond this very place. I cannot help you find your great city and your new king. East of here, two hours journey, in a small village, lives a holy man and woman who can direct you to any place you wish to go. I am sorry that I can not be of more help."

"Dear woman," the tallest king said, "you have been of great help to us. God bless you."

As they began to leave, the smallest of the rulers turned and said, "When we find the new king we will not only offer him gold, frankincense, and myrrh, but we will offer him our lives. Would you like to join in our procession and worship the new king?"

"*No!*" The words came out in a gasp. "I can't leave my home to follow a star in search of a baby!" It seemed like a crazy suggestion. Babouschka turned on her heel and went inside where it was warm and cozy. That night she did not sleep well. She paced the floor and thought and prayed. At daybreak she was certain that God was leading her toward the child. "This could be the greatest moment of my life. I must not miss it," she thought. Still, it took her two more days before she finally decided to try to catch up with the procession. Carrying all her possessions on her back, she left in the direction the kings had traveled. In less than two hours she arrived in the village to the east of her home and approached the home of the holy man and holy woman. The couple pointed her in the direction the procession had traveled. "Would you like something to eat before you continue on your journey?" the woman asked.

"No," Babouschka said. "I must hurry and catch them."

In the days that followed, Babouschka hurried from one village to another. She had never traveled this far before. Each time she came to a new town she asked the same question: "Have you seen a great procession led by three kings?" Each time the answer was the same, "They passed by here two days ago." Finally the answer was different.

"Have you seen a great procession led by three kings?"

"Nobody has been by here in days."

Babouschka was shocked. "I must have taken a wrong turn. Now I may never find the new king." She sat on the ground and wept. Then suddenly she arose and set out with new determination. As she traveled she asked about the great procession. Little by little she learned not only about the procession, but about the birth of the king himself.

"Your new king was born in a manger outside the city of Bethlehem, in Israel," an old woman told her. "It is said that it was the most special night in all the world. Angels sang mysterious and wonderful songs. They announced the birth to shepherds, saying that the new baby was the child of God."

Through these people Babouschka learned that the three kings did find the baby, although they did not arrive on the night of his birth. A star had led them to the place where the child was born. She became even more determined to get to Bethlehem.

Then one day she met a man who had bad news. "It is said that Herod tried to kill the child by slaughtering all of the baby boys in the land. The family escaped with the baby. They have named him Jesus. No one knows where they fled."

Once again Babouschka was disappointed. She was pleased that Jesus was safe but hurt that she was not able to see the child. Perhaps she should turn about and head home to her hut. She was not long in deciding. Once again she set out on a journey to discover the new king.

People in Russia say that Babouschka continues that journey to this very day. She walks all over Russia, entering every home where there is a child. She pushes back the nursery curtains and peers at the babies, hoping to find the one who was born to be king.

Sometimes you will hear a conversation like this. A young child will run to his grandmother and say, "I heard someone outside my bedroom. It sounded like an old lady."

The grandmother will reply, "It was just Babouschka. She is searching for the Christ child and wanted to look in your room. Go back and look around. She may have left you a small present."

When the child returns he will find a piece of candy or a small toy. Babouschka, you see, does not bring bicycles like St. Nicholas or beautiful dolls like parents. She brings gifts that she can carry in the pockets of her old apron. They are not expensive, for Babouschka is poor. The children love her very much, and they don't care if the presents aren't large.

For 2000 years Babouschka has been in search of the Christ child. Do you think she will ever find him?

Behold the Man

This story is adapted from a Jewish folktale.

A young convert approached a bishop and said, "I have heard of a young man who seems to have gained control over large crowds. He advocates the breaking of the law, claims to perform miracles, and even says that he speaks directly to God. Some say that he has claimed to be God. Finally, he denounces the rich and members of the clergy."

"I appreciate your willingness to report such a fanatic," replied the bishop. "Unfortunately, we seem to have more of these types of people today than ever before in history. We shall arrest him and charge him with blasphemy and upsetting the public order. If he fails to repent of what he is doing we shall have to put him in prison where he won't hurt innocent people. Of course, we can't arrest him ourselves, but we do have contacts with the law. Tell me his name and I shall see to it that he is arrested."

"Your zeal in these matters is greatly appreciated," the convert said. "I believe he has many names. Most people simply call him Jesus."

Three Holy Men

Leo Tolstoy introduced his version of Three Holy Men *by quoting Matthew 6:7-8. "And in praying do not heap up empty phrases as the Gentiles do; for they think that they will be heard for their many words. Do not be like them, for your Father knows what you need before you ask him." Tolstoy adapted his version of this tale from a Russian folktale, and I have adapted this story from Tolstoy.*

A bishop was traveling on a large boat across a great Russian sea. As the boat sailed along he overheard an old fisherman telling a story about three holy men who lived on an island off in the distance. "I have seen them with my own eyes, your grace," said the fisherman. "Though I had heard about them for years, I had not met them until last year when my boat was driven to their shore by a great wind."

"What are they like?" asked the bishop.

"They are all very old, perhaps over a hundred years. One is small, hunched over, his beard streaked with gray. The second is tall and very strong. He picked up my boat all by himself. The third stands as straight as an oak. His beard is as long and white as the moon. He is a rather gloomy man."

"Did you talk to them?" the bishop inquired.

"They are men of very few words," said the fisherman. "They do almost everything in silence. I understand that they spend most of their day in prayer to God for the sake of both their own souls and the rest of the world."

The bishop stared off in the distance at the tiny speck that had been identified as the home of the three old men. Soon he left the deck where the conversation had taken place and met with the captain. "I want to land on the next island to talk with the three holy men. I realize that this boat can't get me close, but I would like to pay someone to row me." The captain attempted to dissuade the bishop. "I have heard that they are not as holy as they are stupid, your grace," offered the captain. "People who have met them say they can't even utter an intelligent sentence."

When the bishop insisted, the captain made the arrangements. As he sat on a chair on the small boat the bishop could clearly see the island. On a rock overlooking the harbor stood three old men in tattered clothes, holding hands. The tall one was naked, except for a belt of sackcloth. The shorter man was bent over, and the third was dressed in an old cassock.

"I have heard that you are here devoting your life to prayer," said the bishop to the men after he landed. "I have come to visit you and teach you whatever I can."

The old men smiled and remained silent. After looking at each other for a moment, the oldest spoke. "We do not know how to serve God. We only serve and feed each other."

"But how do you pray?" asked the bishop.

Once again the oldest man spoke. "We pray like this: 'Three art thou; three are we; have mercy upon us.' " As soon as he finished speaking all three men raised their eyes to heaven and said in unison, "Three art thou; three are we; have mercy upon us."

"That is all?" the bishop said, smiling.

The men nodded.

"I can teach you a better way," the bishop said softly. "What I teach came directly from our Lord himself. The Scriptures command us to pray like this: 'Our Father who art in heaven.' "

One by one the men repeated the phrase, "Our Father."

The bishop sat upon a rock, while the men sat at his feet. Word by word, phrase by phrase, he taught them the prayer. They stumbled over the most simple words time after time. All day long the instructions continued until all three could repeat the entire prayer. The bishop, tired but pleased, bid them farewell. The three holy men fell to the ground and bowed as he got into the boat. He lifted them up, and left.

As he was being rowed toward the ship, the bishop could hear the three old men reciting the Lord's Prayer over and over. Even as the ship itself pulled away, he could see the men bent over, holding hands, at the shore.

Most of the travelers lay sleeping as the ship, with full sail, continued on to its destination. The bishop, however, was not tired and sat alone in the stern, looking back at the island. As he sat, a light suddenly appeared off in the distance. Perhaps it was a white bird, or a boat with a white sail. The light was fast approaching when the bishop raced to the captain for a telescope. By this time others on board had spotted the same phenomenon and stood at the rail, pointing off in the distance.

Suddenly the helmsman shouted, "It is the old men! They are running after us over the sea as if it were dry land."

It was true. All three moved effortlessly over the water, holding hands and beckoning the ship to stop. Before anyone could drop a sail they pulled to the side of the boat, shouting for the bishop.

"We have forgotten the prayer, O servant of God. We were repeating it until one of us forgot a word. Before we knew it the whole prayer fell apart. Please teach us again."

The bishop crossed himself, leaned over toward the men, and said, "It is you who should teach us to pray, holy men. Whatever your words, God hears you." Dropping to his knees, the bishop bowed his head.

The three holy men turned and headed back to their island. As they walked a radiant light shone brightly on the face of the water.

A Treasure in Krakow

This Jewish folktale is for those people foolish enough to still believe in dreams and visions. May their number increase.

Many years ago, when people still believed in the power of dreams, Isaac, son of Aaron, lived in the Polish city of Krakow. A poor man, Isaac worked long hours each day to support his family. At night, exhausted from his strenuous labor, he slept soundly.

One night Isaac dreamed that he was walking over a bridge in the far-off city of Prague when a voice told him to look in the water for a valuable treasure. The dream was so realistic he could see the treasure box in the crystal clear water. Night after night he dreamed the same dream.

After two weeks, weary from lack of sleep, Isaac walked the three days journey to Prague to see what he could find. He easily located the bridge of his dreams and had begun to look underneath when a policeman hauled him away to the city jail for questioning.

In the interrogation room three large men demanded, "What is a Jew doing under a bridge in the Gentile section of the city?" In desperation he blurted out the truth, telling the men that he was looking for a treasure he had seen in his dreams.

"You stupid Jew," the arresting officer shouted, "do you believe in dreams? I am too smart for such nonsense. Why, for the last two weeks I myself have dreamed that in the city of Krakow, in the home of a peasant, Isaac, son of Aaron, there is a treasure hidden under the stove in the kitchen. Yet you don't see me wasting my time looking for someone and something that doesn't exist."

Roaring with laughter, the other two policemen grabbed the peasant by the coat and threw him into the street. "Go home, foolish dreamer," they shouted.

Isaac, son of Aaron, dusted himself off and walked back to his home in Krakow. There he moved the stove in the kitchen, found the treasure buried there, and lived a long and wealthy life.

The Selfish Giant

Though this story by Oscar Wilde is neither a folktale nor a fable, it is delightful addition to our collection. I have placed it in this chapter because the ending sounds a bit like some of our Christian legends.

Every afternoon, as they were coming from school, the children used to go and play in the Giant's garden.

It was a large lively garden, with soft green grass. Here and there over the grass stood beautiful flowers like stars, and there were 12 peach trees that in the springtime broke out into delicate blossoms of pink and pearl and in the autumn bore rich fruit. The birds sat on the trees and sang so sweetly that the children used to stop their games in order to listen to them. "How happy we are here," they cried to each other.

One day the Giant came back. He had been to visit his friend the Cornish ogre and had stayed with him for seven years. After the seven years were over he had said all that he had to say, for his conversation was limited, and he determined to return to his own castle. When he arrived he saw the children playing in the garden.

"What are you doing here?" he cried in a very gruff voice, and the children ran away.

"My own garden is my own garden," said the Giant. "Anyone can understand that, and I will allow nobody to play in it but myself." So he built a high wall all round it and put up a notice-board:

TRESSPASSERS WILL BE PROSECUTED

He was a very selfish Giant.

The poor children had now nowhere to play. They tried to play on the road, but the road was very dusty and full of hard stones, and they did not like it. They used to wander round the high walls when their lessons were over and talk about the beautiful garden inside. "How happy we were there!" they said to each other.

Then the Spring came, and all over the country there were little blossoms and little birds. Only in the garden of the Selfish Giant was it still winter. The birds did not care to sing in it as there were no children, and the trees forgot to blossom. Once a beautiful flower put its head out from the grass, but when it saw the notice-board it was so sorry for the children that it slipped back in the ground again and went off to sleep. The only people who were pleased were the Snow and the Frost. "Spring's forgotten this garden," they cried, "so we will live here all year round." The Snow covered up the grass with her great white cloak, and the Frost painted all the trees silver. Then they invited the North Wind to stay with them, and he came. He was wrapped in furs, and he roared all day about the garden, and blew the chimney pots down. "This is a delightful spot," he said. "We must ask the Hail on a visit." So the Hail came. Every day for three hours he rattled on the roof of the castle til he broke most of the slates, and then he ran round and round the garden as fast as he could go. He was dressed in grey, and his breath was like ice.

"I cannot understand why the Spring is so late in coming," said the Selfish Giant as he sat at the window and looked out at his cold, white garden. "I hope there will be a change in the weather."

But the Spring never came, nor the Summer. The Autumn gave golden fruit to every garden, but to the Giant's garden she gave none. "He is too selfish," she said. So it was always winter there, and the North Wind and the Hail, and the Frost, and the Snow danced about through the trees.

One morning the Giant was lying awake in bed when he heard some lovely music. It sounded so sweet to his ears that he thought it must be the King's musicians passing by. It was really only a little linnet singing outside his window, but it was so long since he had heard a bird sing in his garden that it seemed to him to be the most beautiful music in the world. Then the Hail stopped dancing over his head, and the North Wind ceased roaring, and a delicious perfume came to him through the open casement. "I believe Spring has come at last," said the Giant, and he jumped out of bed and looked out.

What did he see?

He saw a most wonderful sight. Through a little hole in the wall the children had crept in, and they were sitting in the branches of the trees. In every tree that he could see there was a little child. And the trees were so glad to have the children back again that they had covered themselves with blossoms, and were waving their arms gently above and twittering with delight, and the flowers were looking up through the green grass and laughing. It was a lovely scene, only in one corner it was still winter. It was the farthest corner of the garden, and in it was standing a little boy. He was so small that he could not reach up to the branches of the tree, and he was wandering all around it, crying bitterly. The poor tree was still covered with frost and snow, and the North Wind was blowing and roaring above it. "Climb up, little boy!" said the Tree, and it bent its branches down as low as it could, but the boy was too tiny.

And the Giant's heart melted as he looked out. "How selfish I have been!" he said. "Now I know why the Spring would not come here. I will put the poor little boy on the top of the tree, and then I will knock down the wall, and my garden shall be the children's playground for ever and ever." He was really sorry for what he had done.

So he crept downstairs and opened the front door quite softly and went out into the garden. But when the children saw him they were so frightened that they all ran away, and the garden became winter again. Only the little boy did not run, for his eyes were so full of tears that he did not see the Giant coming. And the Giant stole up behind him and took him gently in his hand, and put him up into the tree. And the tree broke at once into blossom, and the birds came and sang on it, and the little boy stretched out his two arms and flung them round the Giant's neck and kissed him. And the other children, when they saw that the Giant was not wicked any longer, came running back, and with them came the Spring. "It is your garden now, little children," said the Giant, and he took a great axe and knocked down the wall. And when people were going to market at 12 o'clock, they found the Giant playing with the children in the most beautiful garden they had ever seen.

All day long they played, and in the evening they came to the Giant to bid him good-bye.

"But where is your little companion?" he said, "The boy I put into the tree?" The Giant loved him best because he had kissed him.

"We don't know," answered the children. "He has gone away."

"You must tell him to be sure and come tomorrow," said the Giant. But the children said that they did not know where he lived and had never seen him before, and the Giant felt sad.

Every afternoon, when school was over, the children came and played with the Giant. But the little boy whom the Giant loved was never seen again. The Giant was kind to all the children, yet he longed for his first little friend and often spoke of him. "How I would like to see him." he used to say.

Years went over, and the Giant grew very old and feeble. He could not play about any more, so he sat in a huge armchair and watched the children at their games and admired his garden. "I have many beautiful flowers," he said, "but the children are the most beautiful flowers of all."

One winter morning he looked out of his window as he was dressing. He did not hate the Winter now, for he knew that it was merely the Spring asleep, and that the flowers were resting.

Suddenly he rubbed his eyes in wonder and looked and looked. It certainly was a marvelous sight. In the farthest corner of the garden was a tree quite covered with lovely white blossoms. Its branches were golden, and silver fruit hung down from them, and underneath it stood the little boy he had loved.

Downstairs ran the Giant in great joy, and out into the garden. He hastened across the grass and came near to the child. And when he came quite close, his face grew red with anger, and he said, "Who hath dared to wound thee?" For on the palms of the child's hands were the prints of two nails, and the prints of two nails were on the little feet.

"Who hath dared to wound thee?" cried the Giant. "Tell me that I may take my big sword and slay him."

"Nay," answered the child, "but these are the wounds of Love."

"Who art thou?" asked the Giant, and a strange awe fell on him, and he knelt before the little child.

And the child smiled on the Giant and said to him, "You let me play once in your garden, today you shall come with me and play in my garden, which is Paradise."

And when the children ran in that afternoon, they found the Giant lying dead under the tree, all covered with white blossoms.

John Wesley

This story was prepared for a Protestant church that was unfamiliar with the life and work of John Wesley. The occasion of the 200th anniversary of the Methodist church in 1984 prompted me to acquaint my congregation with "The Methodist Revival."

Eighteenth-century England was ripe for an awakening. What was soon to be called "The Methodist Revival" brought warmth, piety, and zeal to a church mired in lethargy.

John Wesley, the leader and founder of the Methodist church, was the 15th child born to Samuel and Susannah Wesley. Brother Charles, the great hymn writer, was the 18th child in a family of 19. Both grandfathers had been involved in the Puritan reform movement of the 17th century. The father, Samuel, was a priest of the Church of England, and their mother was a spiritual tower of strength. Susannah was no doubt the most powerful religious influence in the life of all her children.

When John was six he was saved from a fire that destroyed his family's home. Dramatically, a neighbor stood on the shoulders of a friend and grabbed John from a second story window just moments before the building collapsed. Samuel Wesley called to all who were watching the fire, "Come, neighbors, let us kneel down. Let us give thanks to God. He has given me all my children. Let the house go. I am rich enough."

As time passed John Wesley believed he had been saved for a purpose. Quoting the Old Testament book of Zechariah, he said, "I was a brand plucked out of the fire."

At age 17, John Wesley enrolled at Christ College, Oxford. Four years later he was ordained a deacon. At Oxford he mastered Greek, German, French, Italian, and Spanish, and developed an appetite for knowledge that was never satisfied. Most significantly, however, John began to read devotional literature and developed a deep desire to lead a holy life. Through the writings of Thomas a Kempis and William Law he began to seek "purity of intention." True religion, he believed, included a significant experience of the heart, not just a confession of the lips.

In 1775 John went home for two years to assist his ailing father in his parish at Epworth. When he returned to Oxford, he became involved with a group formed by brother Charles. Initially the group existed for educational purposes. As John became involved and assumed leadership, the group, soon known as The Holy Club, began to concern itself with spiritual improvement. "Religion that is pure and undefiled before God and the Father is this," wrote the author of James, "To visit orphans and widows in their affliction, and to keep oneself unstained from the world." That pretty well summed up the activities of The Holy Club. In addition to continued prayer and praise in their meetings, the group regularly visited prisoners, particularly those under the sentence of death. With the exception of John Howard, the great prison reformer of the 18th century, John Wesley knew more about the inside of the jails than any man of his time.

Though the term *Methodists* was coined by their detractors, it was a most apt description of the very orderly Holy Club members and their leader. Wesley is not only remembered for his remarkable God-consciousness but is hailed for his administrative and organizational genius. Every hour of the day had its alloted task in his life. Every program he began was tightly monitored. Even in the mundane things of life he could not stand to have anything at loose ends.

In 1735 John Wesley left for the American colony of Georgia with dreams of converting the Indians and establishing The Holy Club among the "noble savages." The dream soon became a nightmare. In many ways the Georgia experience was a crushing failure, perhaps the low point of his life. Not only was he denied the opportunity to preach to the Indians by Governor Oglethorpe, he did not even relate well to the colonists. Later, John barely escaped a damaging situation when he refused to commune a woman who had just recently rejected his proposal of marriage.

Though there may have been valid grounds for his denial, it was seen as a petty and jealous act by the colonists.

Still, the Georgia trip was a turning point in his life. Wesley had long sought total devotion to God and felt as if he had reached his goal. On the trip to Georgia he came into contact with Moravian missionaries who seemed to possess the spiritual commitment he so desperately desired. He witnessed the serenity of the Moravian women and children in the midst of a life-threatening storm and was enchanted with their spiritual zeal.

Back in England, Peter Bohler, another Moravian, counseled the searching Wesley to "Preach faith until you have it and then because you have it you will preach faith." Wesley followed his teacher's advice. On May 24, 1738, Wesley went, with some reluctance, to a meeting on Aldersgate Street where the leader was reading from Martin Luther's Preface to the Epistle to the Romans. Wesley's journals describe the evening. "About a quarter before nine, while he was describing the change God works in the heart through faith in Christ, I felt my heart strangely warmed. I felt I did trust Christ, Christ alone for salvation."

No one ever sought assurance of salvation more urgently than John Wesley. Finally, like Luther before him, when he stopped trying to do things on his own and simply accepted the gift of God, the very thing he sought—assurance—came. He discovered he was no longer a slave in the kingdom, he was a son. The Aldersgate experience marked another turning point in Wesley's life. For the next 52 years he preached salvation by faith throughout the British Isles. His was a message announcing the pure grace of God in Jesus Christ. He seized every opportunity to help people discover the riches of God.

If the Wesleys were excited about their recent experience (Charles had preceded his brother in an "evangelical conversion"), the churches in England were not. Along with their friend George Whitefield, England's most dynamic preacher, the Wesleys were denied access to English pulpits. However, if it seemed as if the

Church of England had closed a door to the "Methodists," it soon appeared that God was opening another.

Denied opportunities to preach indoors, George Whitefield began to preach outdoors to miners as they got off work and to other common people. The response was so overwhelming that he invited John to join him. In March of 1739, John preached to 3000 people at Bristol. A new movement had begun. Soon the Wesleys and George Whitefield were preaching to enthusiastic crowds all over the London area. John felt he would never have a parish again. That was not so bad, for he discovered that, in his words, "The world is my parish."

The outdoor preaching movement quickly grew. In June of 1739 an old foundry that could seat 1500 was rebuilt, and it served both as a preaching place and the Wesley headquarters for the next 38 years. When The Foundry no longer was sufficient to meet the needs of the organization, the City Road Chapel was built just 200 yards away.

Wesley was not a great innovator. He seldom developed a new idea on his own. He was a genius, however, at recognizing a good idea when someone else presented it. Still, most of his "Methodist" ideas developed out of necessity as he found one road after another blocked by circumstances.

In late 1739, a group of people asked Wesley to meet with them for weekly prayer and counsel. The group began with 12 men and soon grew to over 100. From this group The Methodist Society of England developed. Soon a number of small societies sprang up.

When it was necessary to raise money to pay for The Foundry, men were divided into groups of 12 in order to collect a penny a week. This group of 12, called a "Class," was soon used as a means for special guidance and prayer. Wesley knew the groups needed leadership, so he met each Tuesday with one from each group to equip them for their meeting later in the week.

When Wesley could not find qualified ordained clergy from the Church of England to preach at all the places that requested speakers, he was forced to turn to "lay ministers." What began with a single request from Thomas Maxwell turned into an entire society of over 700 who carried the message of salvation by faith throughout England, Ireland, Scotland, and later to the United States. All that was required was a call from God. When Mary Bosanquet declared that she had a call from God, Wesley approved her; thus began the use of women preachers, another innovation he had not foreseen.

Not everyone welcomed the "New England Revival." Opposition from the established Church of England quickly surfaced, and the Methodist preachers often encountered hostile crowds in their open air meetings. Occasionally people became violent and hurled both words and stones at the tiny preacher (Wesley stood 5 feet 4 inches and weighed 125 pounds). Many times John was hit, and once he was even left for dead in an alley.

Wesley became a master at dealing with the hostility. He learned to defuse the people's anger by looking them directly in the eyes and even walking into their midst and confronting their leaders.

Though faced with hardships and criticism, the movement spread beyond England to the colonies, where, under the leadership of Francis Asbury, it found fertile soil.

Throughout his life Wesley remained a loyal member of the Church of England. He believed he had only formed societies, not a rival church. The societies were intended to reform the church and lead people to Christ. During his lifetime the hours of the Methodist services were arranged so as to not conflict with those of the established church. Methodist preachers did not administer sacraments because John assumed that society members would receive the sacraments of Holy Communion and Baptism from the Anglican Church.

Nearly every minute of Wesley's long life was carefully planned. For 60 years he always rose at 4:00 A.M. and almost always went to bed promptly at 10:00 P.M. For 50 years he preached at 5:00 A.M. He learned to use every small piece of the day for learning and prayer. He read and wrote while riding horseback. How did he do it? "I rode with slack rein," he explained. In the more than 40 years he spent on horseback, Wesley traveled more than a quarter of a million miles and preached 42,000 sermons.

His incredibly disciplined life allowed him time to write history books on England and Rome as well as volumes on logic and health. He prepared grammars on Greek, French, and English and completed an excellent English dictionary. He even wrote hymns, though brother Charles was the master hymn writer, penning more than 6000 hymns of beautiful poetry, often for an illiterate public.

In 1784, unable to find priests to administer the sacraments to the large number of American converts, Wesley ordained the first Methodist pastor, Thomas Cooke. It was a reluctant but necessary step for mission work in the New World. It was, of course, both a break with the Church of England and the beginning of the Methodist Church in the United States.

At age 77, Wesley's vigor remained. He rode 100 miles in 48 hours, a feat he duplicated 10 years later. He complained at 83 that he could not write for more than 15 hours without hurting his eyes. At 86 he traveled throughout Ireland for nine weeks, preaching 100 sermons in 60 towns, often in the open air.

Though we will remember him for his writing and his vigorous stands on social issues (he was very vocal in his opposition to slavery), Wesley will be best remembered for his organizational genius and his passion to know and experience the love of God. "We are saved by faith," he declared thousands of times. "God is gracious and loving." This message and his fervent desire for people to live righteous lives is a word that the church in our own day still needs to hear.

5

STORIES OF WISDOM AND FOOLISHNESS

The Milk Cow

A farmer had a cow who gave one pail of milk each day. The man invited guests for a party. In order to save his milk for the special occasion, he refrained from milking the cow for 10 days. He expected that on the last day the cow would give 10 pails of milk. When he went to milk the animal he found she had dried up and gave less milk than ever before.

God Blesses the Children of Eve

"For as in one body we have many members, and all the members do not have the same function, so we, though many, are one body in Christ, and individually members one of another" (Romans 12:4-5).

This story was adapted from a German folktale collected by Jacob and Wilhelm Grimm.

When Adam and Eve were expelled from paradise, they had to build a house for themselves on barren soil and earn their bread by the sweat of their brows. Adam hoed the fields and Eve spun wool. Every year they had a child.

As the years passed the children grew and numbered 14. One day there was a knocking at the door. Adam opened the latch and the heavenly Father stepped in. Eve quickly invited the Lord to sit down. "Thank you," he said as he was offered something to drink. "Are the children here?"

Quickly Adam called the children and seven of them marched into the room and stood politely in front of the Lord. He arose, smiled, and said, "I would like to give each of you a blessing." They knelt before him as he placed his hands on their heads. To the first he said, "You will become a mighty king." Turning to the second, he said, "You will be a princess." The third child heard the Lord say, "You will be a count." Each of the remaining also received his blessing to become scholars and merchants.

When Adam and Eve saw how marvelously God blessed their children, they ran out and found all of the others. In trooped the last seven, out of breath. Again the Lord smiled and said, "I would also like to give my blessing to these children." Adam and Eve smiled in anticipation.

Reaching the first, the Lord said, "You will be a domestic servant." To the second, "You shall become a farmer." The third received the blessing to be a shoemaker. Others were blessed to become blacksmiths, tanners, and seamstresses.

When Eve heard the blessings for the last group, she cried, "Lord, this is not fair. You distribute your blessings so unequally. All of these are my children, and yet you have made some to be kings and some servants!"

God listened to Eve and replied, "Eve, you do not understand. It is necessary for me to provide for all of the tasks on earth through your children. If all were kings and princesses there would be no one to farm or provide food. If all were counts, who would provide clothing? Everyone serves a different function, and in my eyes they are all important and necessary. Like the parts of the body, all blend together and nourish each other."

Then Eve answered, "O Lord, forgive me. I was too hasty in arguing with you. I want your divine will to be done for all my children."

The Jug of Water

This story is adapted from an African folktale.

A Nigerian tribal chief sent out his messengers to invite all of the men of the tribe to a great feast. "All of the food will be provided," they announced, "but each man must bring one jug of palm wine."

Ezra wanted to attend the great festival very much, but he had no wine. He paced the floor trying to think of a solution for his dilemma. Finally his wife suggested, "You could buy a jug of wine. It is not too expensive for such a great occasion."

"How foolish," Ezra cried, "to spend money when there is a way to go free." Once again he paced until he came upon a plan. "Rather than wine I will carry water in my jug. Several hundred men will attend the festival. What will it hurt to add one jug of water to the great pot of wine?"

On the day of the feast the tribal drums began to beat early in the morning, reminding the people of the great festival. All of the men came dressed in their finest clothes, gathering by midmorning at the home of the chief. As each man entered the tribal grounds, he poured his jug of wine into a large earthen pot. Ezra carefully poured the contents of his container into the pot, greeted the chief, and joined the dancers.

When all of the guests arrived, the chief commanded the music to cease and ordered the servants to fill everyone's glass with wine. As the chief spoke the opening words of the festival, all of the guests raised their glasses and drank. Suddenly a cry of disbelief arose from the crowd, and they quickly drank again. What they tasted was not wine, but water. Each guest had decided that his one jug of water could not spoil the great pot of palm wine.

The Dancing Bear

This fable is based on a story by Christian Gellert, an 18th-century German writer.

A Bear was proud of his ability to dance. One day he tried a new step. After a short time he performed for the Monkey and asked, "What do you think of my new dance?"

The Monkey was quick with his review. "It is very bad."

"You are very cruel," the Bear said sadly. "I have only been practicing the dance for a few days. Don't you like the way I swing my arms?"

The Pig, who had been listening to the conversation, interrupted, "Bravo! You are doing well. I have never seen a finer dancer."

The Bear immediately reconsidered the Monkey's words. "I must practice more before I perform again," he thought. "I felt bad when the Monkey criticized me, but I must not be good if the Pig praises me."

It is bad if a wise man does not approve, but if a fool applauds, it is worse.

The Proof of Creation

The heavens declare the glory of God; the skies proclaim the work of his hands" (Psalm 19:1 NIV).

One day an unbeliever began to argue with a religious teacher about God. "You believe many things that cannot be proved," the skeptic said angrily. "For example, who created the world?"

"God," was the teacher's simple reply.

"Can you prove it?" the man shouted.

"Certainly, but first I have a question for you. What are you wearing?"

"What a foolish question!" the skeptic said. "It is a suit!"

"Who made it?"

"The tailor."

"Prove it," the teacher demanded.

"You are even more foolish than I thought," the man exploded, "if you do not know that a tailor makes the clothes we wear."

"And you, my friend," the teacher countered, "are equally foolish if you do not see the hand of God in creation. Just as the house attests to the hand of the builder and the garment to the tailor, so the earth and the order of creation testifies to a higher being. 'The heavens declare the glory of God; the skies proclaim the work of his hands.' "

The Messengers of Death

This German tale is one of many in folk literature that focuses on people who temporarily outwit Death.

A giant was once traveling along a highway when a stranger stepped before him. "Halt!" cried the little man.

"Who are you to give me orders?" laughed the giant as he began to walk past the stranger.

"I am Death," declared the man. "My orders are obeyed by everyone in the world." He moved to a small incline, allowing his words to sink in. Quickly the giant swung his mighty arm, sending Death to the ground unconscious. Satisfied that his opponent could do him no more harm, the giant walked away.

When Death finally awoke he was unable to move. "If I do not get about," he thought, "the world will soon be overcrowded." Just then a young man approached whistling a tune.

When he saw the stranger lying in the road, he stopped to assist him. Tenderly he bathed Death's wounds and gave him a drink from his canteen. Soon the little man was able to stand.

"You do not recognize me?" Death inquired

"I do not know you," said the young man.

"I am Death. I spare no one; I make no exceptions. However, in order to show my gratitude I will not call your name until I have sent my messengers to give you fair warning."

The young man was pleased that he would live safe from the fear of Death. He continued to live a happy and carefree life.

But youth and health did not last long. As the years passed illnesses and pains tormented him by day and gave him little rest by night. "I may be sick, but I will not soon die," thought the man. "Death has not yet sent his messengers. I only wish the pain and suffering were over." One illness followed another. His days were uncomfortable and the road to recovery long.

Finally his health was restored, and the man began to live joyfully again. "I will live a long time," the man thought. "Death still has not sent his messengers."

Then shortly after his health had returned, the man heard someone call his name. When he turned he saw Death standing beside him. "Follow me! Your hour of departure from this world has come."

"What!" cried the man. "You are going to break your word? You promised to send your messengers before you arrived. No one has warned me."

"I am surprised you did not recognize my servants," Death replied. "I sent Fever to slow you down. Next Arthritis came attacking your joints and warning you that any step might be your last. Later Gout gave you aches and pains all over your body. Finally I sent Sleep to remind you each night that Death was near."

The man had no answer. He yielded to his fate and went away with Death.

Heaven and Hell

One day God visited a special old saint. "You have been a faithful follower of mine all these years," God said. "Is there anything that still puzzles you about my kingdom?"

"Yes," the saint confessed. "Although I have read all of the words of Scripture, I still have no idea what heaven and hell are like. I would be deeply grateful if you help me understand."

"Normally I do not answer questions that belong to the realm of mystery," God said, "but since you have led such an exemplary life, I will give you a preview of the world to come."

In the twinkling of an eye the woman was transported through time and space until she found herself standing before the gates of hell. It was not at all what she expected. As she walked through the magnificent black gates, the old saint was struck with the beauty of the place. Ahead of her she saw a huge banquet room with long tables filled with food. It was the most delicious food she had ever seen.

All of the residents of hell were seated about the tables. They all looked normal except for one very important difference. All of the people had very large arms, nearly six feet in length. At the end of each arm was a fork, but the people were unable to eat because no one had an elbow. Even though all of the food was so close at hand, they were unable to put the forks into their mouths. The sounds of hell were not very pleasant, for the people cried out in agony.

Suddenly the woman was transported to heaven. Ahead of her were gleaming white gates. When she walked into the celestial city she was surprised to see that things looked very much like they did in hell. Ahead of her was a banquet table, quite similar to the one she had seen moments before. The food looked amazingly similar.

As the woman walked closer to the table, she could see that people were built identically to those in hell. All had long arms with no elbows, and forks at the end. The sounds in heaven, however, were very different. People were laughing and singing, for they found their long arms to be no great disadvantage. Each person simply loaded his or her fork and then reached out across the table to a friend. The situations were identical except for this one thing: in heaven people fed each other.

The Grain of Rice

Many listeners find parallels between this tale from India and Jesus' parable of the talents in Matthew 25:14ff.

Once there was a good king who ruled wisely and who ruled well. He was loved by all the people of his kingdom. One day the king called his four daughters together and told them that he was leaving on a long journey. "I wish to learn about God. I will spend a long time in prayer. In my absence I will leave the four of you in charge."

"Oh, father," they cried, "don't leave us. We will never be able to rule the kingdom without you."

The king smiled. "You will do well in my absence. Now, before I leave I wish to give each of you a gift. It is my prayer that this gift will help you learn the meaning of rule." The king placed a single grain of rice in each daughter's palm. Then he left.

The oldest daughter immediately went to her room. She tied a long golden thread around the grain of rice and placed it in a beautiful crystal box. Every day she picked up the box and looked at it.

The second daughter also went to her room, where she placed the grain of rice in a wooden box and put it in a secure spot, under her bed.

The third daughter, a very pragmatic young woman, looked at the grain of rice and thought, "This grain of rice is no different from any other grain of rice." She simply threw the grain of rice away.

The youngest daughter took the grain of rice to her room and wondered about the significance of the gift. She wondered for a week, then a month. When nearly a year had passed, she understood the meaning of the gift.

Months turned into years, and the four daughters ruled in the absence of their father. Then, one day, the king returned. His beard was full and his eyes sparkled with illumination gained through years of prayer. The king greeted each of his daughters, and then asked to see the gifts he had left them.

The oldest daughter rushed to her room and brought the crystal box. "Father," she began, "I carefully tied a golden thread around the grain of rice and have kept it near my bed where I have looked at it every day since you left."

Bowing to his daughter, the king accepted the box and said, "Thank you."

Next, the second daughter presented her father with a grain of rice. "All these years I have kept the rice secure under my bed," she said. "Here it is."

Again the father bowed, accepted the box, and said, "Thank you."

The third daughter rushed to the kitchen, found a grain of rice, ran back and said, "Father, here is a grain of rice."

Smiling, the king accepted the grain of rice, bowed, and said, "Thank you."

Finally the youngest daughter stepped before her father and spoke. "I do not have the grain of rice that you gave me," she said.

"Whatever did you do with it?" the king inquired

"Father, I thought about that grain of rice for nearly a year before I discovered the meaning of the gift. I realized that the grain of rice was a seed, so I planted it in the ground. Soon it grew, and from it I harvested other seeds. I then planted all of those seeds, and again I harvested the crop. Father, I have continued to do this. Come, look at the results."

The king followed his daughter to the window where he looked out at an enormous crop of rice stretching as far as the eye could see. There was enough rice to feed their entire small nation.

Stepping before his daughter, the king took off his golden crown and placed it on her head. "You have learned the meaning of rule," he said softly.

From that day the youngest daughter ruled the kingdom. She ruled long, and she ruled wisely, and she ruled well.

Feathers in the Wind

A man went to his rabbi with a question. "Rabbi," he said, "I understand almost all of the law. I understand the commandment not to kill. I understand the commandment not to steal. What I don't understand is why there is a commandment against slandering the neighbor."

The rabbi looked at the man and said, "I will give you an answer, but first I have a task for you. I would like you to gather a sack of feathers and place a single feather on the doorstep of each house in the village. When you have finished, return for your answer."

The man did as he was told and soon returned to the rabbi to announce that the task was complete. "Now, Rabbi, give me the answer to my question. Why is it wrong to slander my neighbor?"

"Ah," the rabbi said. "One more thing. I want you to go back and collect all the feathers before I give you the answer."

"But Rabbi," the man protested, "the feathers will be impossible to collect. The wind will have blown them away."

"So it is with the lies we tell about our neighbors," the rabbi said. "They can never be retrieved. They are like feathers in the wind."

The Miller, His Son, and Their Donkey

"The simple believes everything, but the prudent looks where he is going" (Proverbs 14:15). This fable is adapted from Aesop's collection.

A miller and his son were traveling to market with their donkey. They had not gone far when they overheard three women at a well. "Have you ever seen anything so strange? Two men are walking when they could ride. Why do people have donkeys?"

Responding to the women, the miller quickly put his son on the back of the animal and continued on the journey. Soon they met two men in the midst of a fierce debate. "I say the present generation shows no respect for its elders," cried the older man. Spying the miller and his son, he continued, "There, that proves what I am saying. The young, healthy lad rides while his old father is forced to walk."

Immediately the father told his son to dismount, and he climbed on the animal's back. They hadn't gone very far when they met a man and his wife walking down the road. "Look at that mean father," the woman exclaimed. "He rides while his little son has to walk."

Embarrassed, the miller took his son by the arm. "Come up here with me. We will both ride on the donkey." Together they rode toward the market. Soon they met a group of men loading hay beside the road. "Shame on you," a fat man cried, "overloading the poor donkey. "Why, the two of you are strong enough to carry that poor animal."

Both the miller and his son quickly got off the animal and walked along until they found a large log. They tied the legs of the donkey together and slipped the log between the animal's legs. Then they attempted to carry it over the bridge that led to the market.

People on the other side of the bridge roared with laughter when they saw two men trying to carry a donkey. The noise so frightened the animal that he kicked loose and fell into the river and drowned.

Duty

There was once a vine that felt unappreciated. People often came and removed its grapes without a single word of gratitude.

One day a priest sat down to rest in the shade near the vine. Taking the opportunity to explain its concern, the vine said, "As you can see, I am a vine. Young men and old women come by and take my ripe grapes without ever saying thank you to me for all my efforts. How can people be so insensitive?"

The priest pondered the question for a moment and then replied, "Perhaps people are insensitive, but in all probability their lack of gratitude comes from a different reason. Just as people expect the sun to shine and the wind to blow, they expect grapes from a vine. They are no doubt under the impression that providing grapes is your duty," the priest said with a wry smile.

The Great Stone Face

Adapted from a tale by Nathaniel Hawthorne, this is a story about stories and their power to transform and shape us.

Nestled at the foot of a lofty mountain range in the northeastern part of the United States lay a beautiful fertile valley. The people of the valley either lived in log farmhouses at the edge of the massive black forest or in the villages sprinkled along the clear stream that tumbled down from the mountains.

To the west, in full view of the entire valley, a giant face was etched in the side of an enormous rock. It was as if a titan had sculptured his own likeness on the precipice. There was the broad arch of the forehead a hundred feet in height, the nose with a long bridge, and the vast lips which, if they could have spoken, would have thundered from one end of the valley to the other. Many believed that the serenity and fertility of the valley was in large part due to the Great Stone Face that continually beamed across the land.

In one of the log huts a widow lived alone with her son, Ernest. Daily the two gazed up at the Great Stone Face. "Mother," Ernest said one day, "if the Face could speak I am certain it would have a kindly voice."

"If an old prophecy should come to pass," the mother replied, "we may yet hear the Face speak." The mother then told her son of a legend passed down from the Indians, murmured by the mountain streams, and whispered by the wind that one day a child born in the valley would grow to be a great and wise man bearing the exact likeness of the Great Stone Face. She told how many had grown weary of waiting and no longer believed the legend. Others, however, held fast to it like a great promise.

Ernest never forgot the story his mother told him. Seldom did a day pass when he did not look up at the Face and think about the person who would come to the valley. Often at the end of a work day he would gaze at the Face for hours. It gave him a sense of comfort and strength, for he saw honesty, love, and justice in the face, virtues he longed to experience.

One day Ernest heard a rumor that a man who was born in the valley and who had made a great fortune was returning to spend his last years in the place of his birth. It was said that the man bore a striking resemblance to the Great Stone Face. His name was Gathergold. Now, I am not certain that this was his real name. Perhaps it was given to him because of his talent of amassing great wealth as a merchant and shipbuilder. What is certain is that his fame had spread over the entire world.

Preparations for the arrival of Gathergold began with a flourish. A famous architect came to help build a mansion made of white marble on the land where Gathergold's parents once farmed.

Everything was custom designed. The finest craftsmen were hired, something unheard of in that tiny valley.

Finally, Gathergold himself arrived in a carriage drawn by four beautiful horses. A huge crowd gathered for the occasion. As the carriage came into view, a great murmur went up. "Look! Here he comes." "He is the exact image of the Great Stone Face!" "The prophecy has come true!"

As the crowd cheered, Ernest looked on in disbelief. Gathergold looked nothing like the figure he watched each evening. His skin was yellow, as if his Midas touch had colored him. He had a low forehead, small sharp eyes, and thin lips. Ernest turned away sadly. As he walked home he looked up at the gentle countenance that beamed across the valley, and for a moment he thought he heard the Face say, "He will come. He will come."

Years passed and Ernest became a young man. Though he was hard working and friendly, few knew him, for he was a quiet person. Though he had no formal education, he read many books. If you asked him, however, he would have told you that his favorite teacher was the Great Stone Face.

By this time Gathergold was dead. All the inhabitants in the valley had long ago conceded that there was little resemblance between him and the Great Stone Face.

It was at this time that the hopes of the people of the valley were raised again. Another native son, known as Old Blood and Thunder, was returning to the valley to make his home. Those who knew the general were ready to testify that he had an uncanny resemblance to the Great Stone Face.

Plans were made for a giant parade to welcome the military hero. Ernest and most of the people of the valley took the day off to watch the parade and cheer for their famous son. Reverend Battleblast began the festivities with a prayer: "Our Father, we give you humble thanks for the great blessings you have so graciously bestowed on this valley. We ask a special blessing on this great man of peace in whose honor we are gathered."

As the general stepped forward, Ernest was blocked by the swirling crowd. Not being the least bit pushy, he waited until the crowd parted before he moved forward to view the great man. Ernest was amazed. Old Blood and Thunder looked nothing like the Great Stone Face, despite the voices in the crowd that declared, "He is the image of the Face." "The prophecy has been fulfilled!"

As the general spoke, Ernest was even more convinced that the hopes of the people were ill-placed. "This is no man of peace like the Great Stone Face," Ernest thought. Ernest failed to identify the gentle wisdom and tender sympathy that he had come to associate with his stone teacher in Old Blood and Thunder. "This is not the man of prophecy," Ernest sighed as he walked toward home.

The years sped by swiftly and tranquilly. Ernest was now a man in his middle years. He had gained a reputation among the people of the valley as a simple-hearted man of great wisdom. Seldom did a day pass when neighbors did not come to him for advice. People began to recognize in him something more than an ordinary man.

By this time people had become disillusioned with Old Blood and Thunder and now awaited another who would fulfill the prophecy. Soon their hopes were placed on a noted politician who had been born in the valley, a man known as Old Stony Phiz. I need not tell you much about him except to say that it was clear in the beginning to Ernest that this was not one who had the moral character of the Great Stone Face.

The years moved on and Ernest grew old. His hair was as white as snow, and wrinkles crossed his forehead and furrowed his cheeks. Time had also engraved deep wisdom in him. Many came from beyond the valley to talk or listen to him. People said, "His knowledge does not come from books; he has talked with angels." To each of his visitors Ernest shared his hope that during his lifetime the Great Stone Face would appear.

One day a great poet came to visit. He was a celebrated man who had heard of the wisdom of this gentle man of the valley. The poet was one whose words sparkled with the divine, whose works were acclaimed throughout the land. Ernest had read his poems; they had stirred his soul.

The day the poet arrived Ernest was reading one of the writer's books. "Good evening, can you give a traveler a night's lodging?" asked the poet.

"Gladly," answered Ernest, who then added, "I don't think I have ever seen the Great Stone Face look so hospitably at a stranger." The two men were quickly engaged in conversation and were equally impressed with each other.

Finally, Ernest asked, "Who are you, my gifted friend?"

Placing his finger on the volume Ernest had been reading, he replied, "I am the author of these poems."

Quickly Ernest searched the face of the poet before gazing sadly at the Great Stone Face. "Why are you so downcast, my wise friend?" asked the Poet.

"All my life I have awaited the fulfillment of a prophecy, and when I read your poems I hoped that it might be fulfilled in you—"

"You are now disappointed as you were with Gathergold, Old Blood and Thunder, and Old Stony Phiz. Yes, Ernest, you must add my name to your illustrious three, for I am not worthy of that great name."

"Why not? Your words have a divine ring," Ernest said.

"Perhaps," replied the poet. "Perhaps there is a far-off echo of a divine song in my writing, but my life has not been so sweet. I have lived in a manner of which I am not proud—" His voice trailed off.

The poet and Ernest sat together in silence for a long time. After the hour of sunset, as was his custom in these later years, Ernest went to talk with a group of people in a small, pleasant nook in the mountains. Ernest normally stood on a small elevation while the others sat or reclined on the grass. Off in the distance the Great Stone face watched.

Ernest began to speak, telling people what was on his mind and heart. His words had power, for they were based on experience and harmonized with the life he had always lived. "Never," thought the poet, his eyes glistening with tears, "have I witnessed a man as powerful as this."

As he listened the poet looked off in the distance at the great Face. Suddenly he threw his arms in the air. "Behold, behold, the Great Stone Face!" he shouted.

Ernest whirled and saw that the poet was looking at him. "Ernest is himself the likeness of the Great Stone Face," the poet exclaimed. All of the people looked first at Ernest and then at the mountain and saw what the poet said was true. The Great Stone Face was in their midst, a man of integrity and love.

And so it came to pass. A man born in the valley had grown to be a great and wise man, bearing the exact likeness of the Great Stone Face. He was a man of peace and justice and love. The prophecy had been fulfilled.

6

STORIES OF PEACE AND JUSTICE

"If you want peace," Pope John XXIII once said, "work for justice." The stories in this chapter explore the relationship between these two great themes. Folktales don't offer solutions to our greatest problems, but they do point out our folly and our foolishness when we fail to work together for peace.

The Wasp's Revenge

There was once a bee who thought it was a great shame that wasps did not make honey. He finally decided it was his lot to teach wasps the skill that had been greatly beneficial to all bees.

A much older and wiser bee heard about his plan and advised, "Wasps are suspicious of bees and will not listen even if you approach in good faith. Wasps believe that bees are their greatest enemies."

"Just because wasps and bees were once enemies, it need not always be so," thought the bee. He then covered himself with yellow pollen until he looked exactly like a wasp.

Presenting himself as a wasp who had just made a great discovery, the bee soon taught wasps the art of making honey. They were delighted and worked hard under his direction. As the days passed the wasps were able to produce as much honey as most bees.

Then one day, under the harsh rays of the sun, the pollen that covered the bee melted, and the wasps realized they had been fooled. Quickly they fell upon the bee and stung him to death. Then, knowing that all bees were enemies, they quickly destroyed all of the honey they had made.

The Otter's Children

"There is no way to peace," a wise man once said, "peace is the way." This Jewish folktale reminds us that if peace is to be experienced, some one must stop the cycle of violence.

The Otter rushed before the king crying, "My lord, you are a man who loves justice and rules fairly. You have established peace among all your creatures, and yet there is no peace."

"Who has broken the peace?" asked the king.

"The Weasel!" cried the Otter. "I dove into the water to hunt food for my children, leaving them in the care of the Weasel. While I was gone my children were killed. 'An eye for an eye,' the Good Book says. I demand vengeance!"

The king sent for the Weasel who soon appeared before him. "You have been charged with the death of the Otter's children. How do you plead?" demanded the king.

"Alas, my lord," wept the Weasel, "I am responsible for the death of the Otter's children, though it was clearly an accident. As I heard the Woodpecker sound the danger alarm, I rushed to defend our land. In doing so I trampled the Otter's children by accident."

The king summoned the Woodpecker. "Is it true that you sounded the alarm with your mighty beak?" inquired the king.

"It is true, my lord," replied the Woodpecker. "I began the alarm when I spied the Scorpion sharpening his dagger."

When the Scorpion appeared before the king, he was asked if he indeed had sharpened his dagger. "You understand that sharpening your dagger is an act of war?" declared the king.

"I understand," said the Scorpion, "but I prepared only because I observed the Turtle polishing its armor."

In his defense the Turtle said, "I would not have polished my armor had I not seen the Crab preparing his sword."

The Crab declared, "I saw the Lobster swinging its javelin."

When the Lobster appeared before the king, he explained, "I began to swing my javelin when I saw the Otter swimming toward my children, ready to devour them."

Turning to the Otter, the king announced, "You, not the Weasel, are the guilty party. The blood of your children is upon your head. Whoever sows death shall reap it."

The Cobbler and the King

Folktales about a good king kindle the yearning we all have to live in a just society. Christians confess Jesus to be King of kings and find parallels in every story that speaks of a ruler who knows his people intimately and cares for their welfare.

This marvelous tale seems to have found a home in Turkey, Greece, Germany, Israel, and other countries. In its present form it states a simple truth: peace grows out of our willingness to trust that God will provide what is needed in life.

There was once a king who ruled his small country with justice and love. Unknown to his subjects, the king would put on a disguise in the evenings and roam the streets of the towns in order to understand life from the perspective of the people.

One night as he walked in disguise, the king was drawn to a simple cottage. The doors and windows of the house were thrown wide open, and inside a rather robust man was eating and singing with great volume. Knocking on the door, the king inquired, "Is a guest welcome here?"

"A guest is a gift from God," the man shouted. "Please, enter and eat with me."

The king sat down and began to eat the very simple but substantial food that rested on the table. The two men talked freely, immediately feeling a bond between them. Finally the king asked, "What is your trade, my friend?"

"I am a cobbler," came the enthusiastic reply. "Each day I take my tool kit and wander about town fixing people's shoes. They give me some pennies, and I put them in my pocket. When the day is over, I spend it all to buy my evening meal."

"You spend all of your money each day?" the king asked incredulously. "Don't you save for the future? What about tomorrow?"

"Tomorrow is in the hands of God, my friend," laughed the cobbler. "He will provide, and I will praise him day by day."

Before the king left that evening, he asked if he might return the next night. "You are always welcome, my friend," the cobbler replied warmly.

On the way home the king developed a plan to test the simple cobbler. The next morning he issued a proclamation prohibiting the repair of shoes without a permit. When he returned the next evening he found the cobbler eating and drinking and making merry. "What have you done today, dear friend?" the king asked, hiding his surprise.

"When I heard that our gracious king had issued a proclamation prohibiting the repair of shoes without a permit, I went to the well, drew water, and carried it to the homes of people. They gave me some pennies, I put them in my pocket, and went out and spent it all on this food," the cobbler sang. "Come, eat, there is plenty for all."

"You spent it all?" the king asked. "What if you cannot draw water tomorrow? Then what will you do?"

"Tomorrow is in the hands of God," the cobbler shouted. "He will provide, and I, his simple servant, will praise him day by day."

The next morning the king decided to test his new friend again. He sent his heralds throughout the land announcing that it was illegal for one person to draw water for another. That evening when he returned to visit the cobbler, he found him eating and drinking and enjoying life as before. "I worried about you this morning when I heard the king's proclamation. What did you do?"

"When I heard our good king's new edict, I went out to chop wood. When I had a bundle I brought it to town and sold it. People gave me some pennies, I put them in my pocket, and when the work day was over, I spent it all on this food. Let us eat."

"You worry me," the king said. "What if you cannot chop wood tomorrow?"

"Tomorrow, good friend, is in the hands of God. He will provide."

Early the next morning the king's heralds announced that all woodchoppers should report immediately to the palace for service in the king's army. The cobbler-turned-woodcutter obediently reported and was trained all day. When evening came, he was given no wages, but he was allowed to take his sword home. On the way home, he stopped at a pawn shop where he sold the blade. Then he bought his food, as usual. Returning to his house, he took a piece of wood, carved a wooden blade, attached it to the sword's hilt, and placed it in his sheath.

When the king arrived that evening, the cobbler told him the entire story. "What happens tomorrow if there is a sword inspection?" the king asked.

"Tomorrow is in the hands of God." answered the cobbler calmly. "He will provide."

In the morning the officer in charge of the palace guard took the cobbler by the arm. "You are to act as executioner today. This man has been sentenced to death. Cut off his head."

"I am a gentle man," the cobbler protested. "I have never hurt another man in my life."

"You will do as you are commanded," the officer shouted.

As they walked to the place of execution, the cobbler's mind was exploding. As the prisoner knelt before him, the cobbler took the hilt of his sword in one hand, raised his other palm to the heavens, and prayed in a loud voice. "Almighty God, you alone can judge the innocent and the guilty. If this prisoner is guilty, let my sword be sharp and my arms be strong. If, however, he is innocent, let this sword be made of wood."

Dramatically, the cobbler pulled his sword from the sheath. The people were amazed to see that the sword was made of wood.

The king, who had watched the events from a distance, ran to his friend and revealed his true identity. "From this day forward you will come and live with me. You will eat from my table. I will be the host and you will be the guest. What do you say about that?"

The cobbler smiled from ear to ear. "What I say is, the Lord has provided, and you and I together will praise him day by day."

An Old Story

A certain rabbi accepted the appointment to a new village only after a great amount of pleading from the people. They promised that he would have ample time for study. He finally agreed to the new appointment with one stipulation: the leaders were not to demand his attendance at public meetings of the town unless they were considering a new custom.

Time passed, and the city council was proposing a new ordinance that would forbid paupers to beg on the streets or to knock on the doors of homes in the village. Instead, they would be given a monthly grant from village funds. A delegation approached the rabbi to ask that he be present when they discussed the new law.

"You promised not to bother me with discussions concerning old regulations," the rabbi protested.

"Dear rabbi," the leader explained, "this is a new piece of legislation."

The rabbi was quick to respond. "There is nothing novel in your proposal. Long ago, in Sodom and Gomorrah, they had a law forbidding people to give alms to the poor."

The proposal was immediately removed from the village agenda.

A Thousand Paper Cranes

In our attempt to make the horror of nuclear war concrete, stories such as this one about a little Japanese girl are a great aid. If you use this story in a setting where there is time for activities and discussion, you may wish to have people fold paper cranes using the instructions at the end of the story. For an illustrated version of this story see Sadako and the Thousand Paper Cranes *by Eleanor Coerr, (Putnam).*

On August 6, 1945, a giant American airplane, the Enola Gay, dropped the world's first atomic bomb on the Japanese city of Hiroshima, killing nearly 100,000 people and ushering in an age of terror for the entire human race. The "Flash," as the people of Hiroshima refer to it, destroyed 4.7 square miles of their city of 250,000 people and could be seen 170 miles away.

Sadako, who was two when the thunderbolt fell two miles from her home, was one of the fortunate ones, her father told her. Only six of their relatives, including their grandmother, Oban Chan, had been killed. Though Sadako could not remember the events of that horrible day, 11 years later she knew the story well. In addition to the words of her father, each year on August

6 the city of Hiroshima celebrated Peace Day. In the atmosphere of a fair, with many wonderful foods and exciting entertainment, Peace Day was an occasion for young and old to remember. They gazed at the pictures of burned people and the devastation of the bomb, which had the power equal to 2000 B-29s fully loaded with conventional weapons. City officials gave speeches and the Buddhist priests released hundreds of white doves that circled the city. Before the day was over people inscribed the names of loved ones who died because of the bomb on paper lanterns that were lit with candles and set adrift on the seven rivers that flow through Hiroshima. The rivers carried the lanterns slowly to the sea, and with them the memories of those who died.

When she was nine years old, Sadako dreamed of being a great runner. With the speed of a deer she had won many races and had been chosen to represent her class at Field Day. "Someday," she thought, "I will represent the Junior High in races." To reach her goal she would have to practice every day. Sadako ran home from school, easily beating her brother. At night she ran through the streets. With each passing day it seemed that Sadako became stronger and faster.

Then one day Sadako fell. While running, she had become dizzy. It was nothing to worry about, so she said nothing. As the days passed, the dizziness came more often. Then one day at school she fell and was unable to stand. Her teacher called her parents who rushed her, against her will, to the hospital. She sensed the fear of her mother as she entered the doctor's office. A few hours later Sadako heard the most frightening phrase in Hiroshima—atomic poisoning. Leukemia, or cancer of the blood, was a result of the radiation that was stored in the bodies of people who lived in Hiroshima during the Flash. It was the most feared illness of all. "Daddy," she cried, "I can't have the poison. I wasn't even scratched by the bomb!"

"The doctors aren't certain," her father said sadly. "They simply want to take some tests." But as the days passed, it was clear to

Sadako from the voices and looks of the doctors that something was very wrong. She knew she would be in the hospital for a long time.

Then one day Chizuko, her best friend, came to the hospital with her hands behind her back. "Guess what I have for you," she laughed. Without waiting for an answer she held high in the air a golden piece of paper that had been carefully folded. "A crane!"

Sadako thanked her. "It isn't just a gift, it is a good luck piece," Chizuko cried. "Haven't you heard the story of the crane? It is said the crane lives for a thousand years, and any sick person who folds a thousand cranes will get well. Let's get started!" With that Chizuko began to teach Sadako how to fold the crane out of a scrap of paper.

With the help of her friend Sadako folded several cranes that afternoon. Strangely, she felt better. Perhaps the crane did bring sick people good luck. "I'll have to have more paper," Sadako said. "I still have 990 more to fold."

In the days that followed, Sadako folded many cranes. Her brother and the nurses hung them from the ceiling and put them on every shelf in the hospital room. Everyone saved paper for her. By the time she had folded 200 cranes, the dizziness began to get worse. At times she was so weak that it was impossible to lift her arms. Then suddenly she would have a burst of energy and her hands would quickly fold the beautiful paper cranes again—300—350—400.

Soon the period between cranes became longer for Sadako. She was determined, however, and the total still rose—450—500. Each day the nurses encouraged the bright-eyed little girl with the pleasant smile. "Only a few hundred more to go," they would tell Sadako.

Near the end of July, Sadako folded her 600th paper crane. Her family and friends were told they should keep their visits short. She got weaker every day. Still, each time they visited her in the special hospital for leukemia victims, they discovered she had folded a few more cranes. Now, however, the progress was counted by fives rather than fifties. 610—615—620.

Finally, one night Sadako's strength gave out. She closed her eyes and did not open them again. She had fallen short of her goal.

Chizuko and Sadako's other classmates folded the remaining paper cranes and threaded them into a wreath that was placed over her body. Then, with their teacher's help, Sadako's classmates began to raise money throughout Japan for a children's monument to be placed in Peace Park as a reminder of what the "Flash" had done to children. After a long and difficult campaign, the money was raised and a sculptor hired to design the monument. Today, on a large hollow pedestal of granite, stands the figure of Sadako, a golden crane perched on her outstretched hand. People from all over the world have sent hundreds of crane wreaths that have been draped over the granite figure.

A Folded Crane Club has been formed to assist the *hibakusha*—the survivors of the atomic blast. Members of the club hold memorial services for children who die. They print a newsletter. They also write letters to governments all over the world, urging leaders to work for peace. The memory of Sadako and the symbol of the paper crane have made thousands of people determined to do all they can to insure that no one ever has to suffer from the "Flash" again.

How to fold a paper crane:

1. Fold a *square* piece of lightweight paper in half horizontally. Then fold **A** back to bottom center (**D**), and **B** *forward* to front bottom center (**C**).

2. Your paper should look like this.

3. Pull **C** (the front) and **D** (the back) apart all the way until you have a flat diamond (as in small diagram).

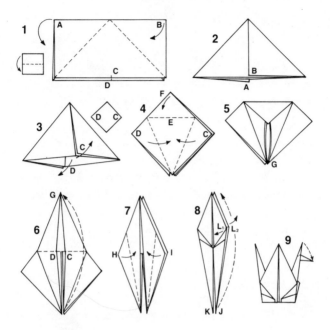

4. Fold top layers of **C** and **D** inward to center line **E** and fold down **F** along dotted line.

5. Your paper should look like this.

6. Now unfold step 4. Take top layer *only* at **G** and pull it up, making use of the crease (dotted line). This allows points **C** and **D** to fold back to the center line along the creases. Turn paper over and repeat steps 4, 5, and 6, ignoring new flap topped by point **G**.

7. With split at bottom, fold **H** and **I** inward so that the edges meet the center line. Turn paper over and repeat.

8. Temporarily open flaps at **L₁** and **L₂**. Pull **J** up to top *between* flaps and close flaps (**L₁** and **L₂**). Repeat with **K**. Fold down head. Fold down wings.

The Heavenly City

This story, adapted from a Jewish folktale, reminds us of the words of Jesus, "The kingdom of God is not coming with signs to be observed; nor will they say, 'Lo, here it is!' or 'There!' for behold, the kingdom of God is in the midst of you" (Luke 17:20-21). In the same way, the vision of peace begins close to us.

There was once a poor man who grew weary of the corruption and hatred that he experienced every day. He was tired of the constant injustice that his people experienced. His family and friends listened as he spoke passionately of his desire for a city where justice was honored and peace experienced. Night after night he dreamed of a land free from discord, a city where heaven touched earth.

One day he announced that he could wait no longer. He packed a meager meal, kissed his family, and set out in search of the magical city of his dreams. He walked all day, and just before the sun set, he found a place to sleep just off the road, in a forest. He ate his sandwich, said his prayers, and smoothed the earth where he would lie. Just before he went to sleep he placed his shoes in the center of the path, pointing them in the direction he would continue the next day.

That night, as he slept, a sly fellow walked that very path and discovered the traveler's shoes. Unable to resist a practical joke, he turned the shoes around, pointing them in the direction from which the man had come.

Early the next morning the traveler rose, said his prayers, ate what remained of the food he had brought, and started his journey by walking in the direction his shoes pointed. He walked all day long, and just before the sun set, saw the heavenly city off in the distance. It wasn't as large as he expected, and it looked strangely familiar. He entered a street that looked much like his own, knocked on a familiar door, greeted the family he found there, and lived happily ever after in the heavenly city of his dreams.

The Wolf and the Farmer

A wolf was eating a sheep when a farmer discovered him and began to beat him with a stick.

The wolf cried, "It is not fair for you to beat me. It is not my fault if I am grey. God made me this way."

The farmer laughed as he hit the wolf again. "I do not beat wolves because they are grey, but because they eat the sheep."

The Woodcutter and the Doves

This story, in its Oriental, Scandinavian, or European versions, suggests that kindness and gentleness are ultimately rewarded, often in surprising ways.

Lars was a woodcutter who had spent his entire life in a huge forest near Trondheim. He knew every trail in the forest. Some said that young Lars might even know every tree and bush.

One day while Lars was getting ready to cut down a tree he heard a cooing sound not far away. He followed the sound and discovered two beautiful white doves caught in a wooden trap.

"Poor birds," Lars thought. "If I don't free them, surely they will die." He quickly opened the trap and let the two white birds fly away. Then the woodcutter returned to his job and forgot about the birds.

In the days ahead, Lars married a beautiful young woman, moved to a small city ten miles away, and began to raise a family. Twenty-five years passed quickly. Though he prospered in his new job, Lars often thought of the forest that had been his early home.

One day Lars rose early in the morning, kissed his wife and children good-bye, and said, "I am going back to the forest. I will return tomorrow for supper."

The ten-mile journey seemed like only a few hundred yards to the eager woodcutter. When he arrived at his beloved forest, everything seemed the same. He recognized the old pathways he had walked upon, as well as the rocks, and even a few of the old gnarled trees.

Lars began to walk deeper and deeper into the forest. After a journey of over an hour, he thought, "The forest has grown much larger; I should be on the other side by now." Still he walked on, farther and farther, until he realized that he was lost. This had never happened to him before. Was it possible that he had also lost his sense of direction? He continued to walk until night came and darkness settled over the forest. Lars was cold, hungry, and, for the first time, frightened in the forest.

Just as the former woodcutter began to prepare a bed for himself, he saw a light in the distance. "Strange, I don't remember anyone living here," he thought.

He followed the light and knocked on the door. After a few moments, the door slowly creaked open. As light from the cabin hit the night air, a chill ran down the woodcutter's spine. Standing in the door was the strangest woman he had ever seen. Her skin was whiter than the snow, and her eyes shone like hot coals. She had long black hair that hung far below her waist.

"Can I help you?" the woman asked in a raspy voice.

"I'm lost," Lars said haltingly. "And I'm hungry—and cold. I also need a place to sleep."

"Come right in," the woman said, beckoning with a long finger.

Lars felt most uncomfortable in this strange house, but he was so hungry, and the food the woman placed before him smelled so good, that he quickly ignored his apprehension. He ate everything that the woman placed before him.

When he finished he stood to thank his hostess. He looked around but couldn't see her. Suddenly there was a hissing sound from the corner of the room, and Lars saw a huge black snake slowly slithering toward him. When the snake reached him it stood straight up on its tail and looked at him. The snake had the face of the old woman.

"Ssssso, you have come at last," hissed the snake. "I have waited 25 years. Do you remember the two white birds that you set free? They were going to be my evening meal. When I saw you release them, I swore that one day I would kill you."

"I did not know they were yours," said the woodcutter. "If you would have said something, I would never have opened the trap."

"Ssssso," the snake said, "you do admit you set them free. Now I know I have the right person. Tonight, at midnight, I will kill you."

"Is there nothing that can save me?" the woodcutter cried.

"Yesssss," the snake said slowly. "If the bell in the old church tower rings 12 times before midnight, you will be free. But since I will not let you leave this house, it is certain that you will be my midnight snack."

Full of panic, Lars looked about the cabin, attempting to find a way to escape. All the windows were bolted, and the snake had moved in front of the only door. There was no way out. He slumped to the floor, realizing that he would soon die.

As he sat on the floor Lars thought of his wife and children. He remembered the joy he had experienced working in the woods. He had been a fortunate man, up to now. Tears ran down his cheeks.

After a long time, the woodcutter looked up at the clock on the wall. It was five minutes before midnight. The snake began to make its way from the doorway toward Lars. It curled itself around the chair in front of him and taunted him with its darting tongue.

Just before the big hand reached the midnight hour there was a weak sound, way off in the distance. It was the sound of a bell. It rang and rang. Lars started counting: nine, ten, eleven, twelve.

With the last peal of the bell, the house vanished, the snake disappeared, and Lars stood alone in the dark forest. Knowing he could go nowhere until morning, he curled up and fell asleep, wondering who had rung the bell and saved his life.

When the first beams of light broke through the leaves, Lars was on his feet. Off in the distance he could make out the outline of an old church. He walked quickly to the building and entered the broken wooden door. He found the stairs to the bell tower and climbed quickly to the top. Peering intently at the old bell, he saw spots of blood. Down below, on the floor of the bell tower, he saw white feathers, more blood, and the two white doves who had thrown their tiny bodies at the bell 12 times, in order to repay the man who had saved their lives.

Lars gently picked up the birds. Though their bodies were bruised and broken, each had a steady heartbeat. He tore his shirt and wrapped each of the birds tenderly in a piece of the cloth. He stayed with the doves, feeding and caring for them, until they were healthy. Then, one morning, he opened the church door and, for the second time, set the two white doves free. When they flew out of sight, he returned to his home, greeted his wife and children, and lived happily ever after.

The Most Trusted Servant

Isak was King Olaf's most trusted friend and advisor. When the royal court was in session, he always stood at the king's right hand.

Few people realized that only a few years before the good king had discovered Isak tending sheep, dressed in a tattered sheepskin jacket and a crude pair of homemade boots. The king had been so impressed with the wisdom and honesty of this simple man that he had given him a job in the royal court. In a matter of only a few months Isak had become the chief servant and treasurer of the king.

Each month Isak brought his master an accounting of all the gold and precious jewels stored in the palace vaults. In addition to jewels, Isak delivered the value of the furnishings of every room in the entire palace, including the state apartments.

There was one exception to his careful accounting, however. Nothing was ever mentioned about the chamber in the topmost tower, the chamber where Isak spent an hour in the middle of each day. In fact, no one knew what lay inside the thick doors of that mysterious room, for Isak was the only one who possessed a key.

One day King Olaf decided to put the members of his royal court to a test. He entered the hall where they all had assembled carrying a large, beautiful pearl.

Summoning the first servant, he asked, "What do you think this pearl is worth?"

"More than 100 wagonloads of gold," the man promptly replied.

"Break it!" commanded the king.

"Impossible, my lord," the servant cried. "The pearl is too valuable to destroy."

"An interesting answer," the king said cautiously.

Olaf turned next to the second servant. "Do you also judge this jewel to be valuable?" he asked.

"I certainly do, my lord," the second servant replied. "It is surely worth half a kingdom."

"Break it," commanded the king.

"To destroy such a thing of beauty would bring dishonor to my king," the servant declared.

"Thank you for your response," the king said softly.

One by one the servants refused to break the magnificent pearl, and, with each refusal, the king became more quiet.

Finally the king turned to Isak.

"What is this pearl worth?" the king asked.

"More than all the gold I have ever seen," answered the king's most trusted servant.

"Break it!" commanded the king.

Quickly Isak moved to a place where there were two large stones, and he crushed the pearl between them. All that remained of the precious gem was a handful of dust.

A storm of protest arose from the servants. "Isak is a madman!" they shouted.

Isak raised his arm and asked to speak. "What is more precious, the pearl or our king's command? Anyone who would put a mere stone before the word of the king lacks true loyalty." When he finished speaking, the other members of the court bowed their heads in shame, while their hearts began to fill with terror. "We have allowed our good sense to be swayed by a piece of stone," they cried. "Our foolishness shall soon cost us our lives!"

The king was pleased that Isak had exposed the foolishness of the other princes of the court. With a wave of his hand he signaled for the executioner to draw his sword.

Immediately Isak prostrated himself before the king. "I beg you, spare the lives of your servants," he cried. "Use this as an opportunity to demonstrate the value of forgiveness."

Deeply moved, the king pardoned all of his servants, who pledged him their eternal loyalty. Strangely, though the members of the royal court were grateful to the king, they were angry with Isak. One by one they vowed to find something that would remove him from the king's favor.

Soon the attention of the courtiers was drawn to Isak's daily trips to the chamber in the topmost tower. "What do you think he has hidden in this secret place?" they asked one another.

"He alone has a key," observed the oldest member of the court.

"I say he is stealing from the king. He uses the chamber to store his gold," said another servant.

Day after day their hearts darkened, until all the servants decided to report to the king. "It is our belief, your grace, that

Isak is stealing gold from you. He is not as trustworthy as it appears."

A small smile fell across the mouth of the king as he addressed his royal court. "I have never asked Isak about his daily trips to this secret room. You have my permission to search the area. Whatever you find is yours to keep."

The servants rushed up the stairs, broke the iron lock, and swarmed into the room greedily, looking for the hidden treasure. What they saw confounded them. The room was entirely bare except for a dusty sheepskin jacket and a tattered old pair of boots.

"He must have hidden the gold," one of the servants cried.

Eager hands began to tear holes in the walls and the ceiling in search of the elusive treasure. After an hour of destruction they had found nothing

Suddenly King Olaf entered the room, followed by Isak. "By this time you must all be rich men," the king said slyly. "Quick, show me the hoarded gold!"

"Forgive us, great king," the servants cried. "We found nothing but an old sheepskin jacket and a tattered pair of boots."

Turning to Isak, the king said with a chuckle, "The treasure you hoard is indeed strange. Suppose you explain the nature of these valuable items to the members of the court."

"When you chose to lift me up to my position in the royal court I had nothing in the world," said Isak. "I knew all that I had came as a gift from you. Without your grace, what am I?"

"Nothing but a shepherd," sneered the servants.

"A shepherd who wears a sheepskin jacket and a homemade pair of boots," Isak agreed. "Each day I return to this room to remember who I am and where I came from. The jacket reminds me that I should not take my present position too seriously. The boots point to the lowliness of my birth. 'A grateful heart,' the psalmist said, 'is the beginning of true worship.' "

Isak bowed before the king. "I am thankful for the trust you have shown in me."

The king smiled. "And I am pleased that you have continued to serve me with a humble heart. I never doubted your fidelity. After the servants repair your room they will place the jacket and the boots where they found them. These simple objects are of far more value than gold or jewels."

Isak lived many years as King Olaf's most trusted servant. When he died, the sheepskin coat and the tattered old boots were placed in the royal treasury, along with the king's precious gems.

---- **7** ----

STORIES OF WEALTH AND GREED

The Miser

Christians understand God to be a spendthrift who gives freely and lavishly to his beloved children. A miserly spirit is therefore opposite of all that God is and all that God has done. Folk literature, like Scripture, views the stingy person as one who is ungrateful to God. Such people are counted as fools.

There was a rich Jew who never gave alms to the poor or contributed to charitable causes. People in his small village never called him by name, they simply referred to him as The Miser.

One day a beggar came to the door of The Miser. "Where do you come from?" he asked.

"I live in the village," answered the beggar.

"Nonsense," cried The Miser. "Everyone in this village knows that I do not support beggars!"

In the same village there lived a poor shoemaker. He was a most generous man who responded to every person in need and every charitable cause that was brought to his attention. No one was ever turned away empty-handed from his door.

One day The Miser died. The village leaders decided to bury him at the edge of the cemetery. No one mourned his passing; no one followed the funeral procession to the place of burial.

As the days passed the rabbi heard disturbing news regarding the shoemaker. "He no longer gives alms to the beggars," complained one man. "He has refused every charity that has approached him," declared another.

"Has anyone asked about his change?" inquired the rabbi.

"Yes," replied the first man. "He says he no longer has money to give away."

Soon the rabbi called on the shoemaker. "Why have you suddenly ceased giving money to worthy causes?"

Slowly the shoemaker began to speak. "Many years ago the man you called The Miser came to me with a huge sum of money and asked me to distribute it to beggars and charities. He made me promise that I would not reveal the source of the money until after he died. Once every month he would visit me secretly and give me additional money to distribute. I became known as a great benefactor even though I never spent a penny of my own money. I am surprised that no one questioned me earlier. How could anyone who earned the wages of a shoemaker give away as much money as I have all these years?"

The rabbi called all of the villagers together and told them the story. "The Miser has lived by the Scriptures, keeping his charity a secret," the rabbi told them. Then they all walked to the grave of The Miser and prayed. When he died the rabbi asked to be buried near the fence, next to the grave of the man known as The Miser.

Painted Gold

This fable, or one quite similar, appears under the authorship of several storytellers, including Aesop.

There was once a miser who sold all of his possessions and bought a large piece of gold. He buried the treasure in the earth near a large wooden fence. Each day he dug up the gold and admired it.

A gardener observed the miser's daily ritual and wondered what the old man was doing. One night he crept to the exact spot where he had seen the miser and discovered the magnificent gold piece. He immediately placed it in his pocket and left the country.

When the miser discovered the empty hole the next day he let out a loud cry of anguish. A neighbor heard the scream and came running to the aid of her friend. Full of grief, the miser told her the entire story.

"Stop your crying," the neighbor advised, "and find a stone of equal size. Paint it the color of gold and put it back in the earth. Each day you can come and pretend that it is still here. The stone will serve the same purpose since you never meant to use the gold anyway."

Elijah and Orpah

This story is adapted from Ilyas, *a story by Leo Tolstoy.*

In the state of Wyoming there was a man by the name of Elijah who farmed with his father. Shortly after Elijah married, his father died, leaving him a modest amount of land and cattle.

Elijah was a good manager and a hard worker. With the help of his wife, Orpah, Elijah was able to increase the amount of land he owned and the size of his herd until he had more than anyone in the entire county.

Elijah developed a reputation for hosting large parties. People came from long distances just to say that they had been at the home of Elijah. He was famous for serving western style barbecue as well as the finest fancy dishes. No matter how many people came, there was always plenty for all.

Orpah and Elijah had two sons and a daughter. While the family was poor, the sons worked diligently in the fields with their father. When they became wealthy, the young men became headstrong and cultivated dangerous and expensive habits. One developed a serious drinking problem, and the other was killed in a brawl. The oldest, the drinker, had an unhappy marriage and often beat his wife. One day his father made a cash settlement with him, and the two parted company.

Shortly after the departure of his son, problems arose. In the spring the cattle were struck with a curious ailment, and most of them died or had to be killed. Most of his cash crop was lost during the worst drought they had experienced in decades. During the fall robbers stole all of his prize horses. Suddenly, with most of his livestock gone, and his cash crop decimated, Elijah was forced to sell everything he owned. All that remained was an old junk car and enough personal items to furnish a small house.

By this time they had lost contact with their son, and their only daughter had died. Elijah and Orpah were too proud to apply for welfare. They were in their early 70s.

A neighbor who admired the couple visited them one day and invited them to live with him. "Elijah, there is always plenty of machinery that needs fixing, and you are still an excellent mechanic. You need not do the heavy work. Orpah, you can help feed chickens and be in charge of my large garden in the summer. I will provide you with a simple cottage and ample food to meet your needs."

Elijah and Orpah thanked their neighbor and began immediately to live and work as hired laborers. At first the work was hard, but they soon adapted. The landlord was pleased for they knew what needed to be done and worked without prodding.

One day guests arrived at the ranch of the landlord. Elijah was asked to supervise the slaughter of a young calf, and Orpah to be in charge of the barbecue. The guests were gathered under a large tent top to shade them from the hot Wyoming sun. As they ate and drank, Elijah, just finished with his work, passed by in the distance, on the way to his cottage.

"Do you see that man?" the owner asked the group. "He was once the richest man in this section of Wyoming. Perhaps you've heard of him; his name is Elijah."

"Of course I have heard of him," said one of the guests. "I've never met him, but his reputation has reached far beyond the county."

"Today he is penniless," the owner said. "He lives with me as a laborer."

"Life is like a ferris wheel," one of the guests said, "lifting some people up, and dropping others down. Tell me, is the old man sad?"

"He doesn't appear sad. He lives quietly with his wife and is a very hard worker."

"Could we speak to him?" another guest asked. "It would be interesting to learn about his life."

"I will call him, but be careful. He is a proud man." Walking a few paces toward the cottage, the owner shouted, "Elijah, bring Orpah and join us for a drink!"

Soon Elijah and Orpah came. They greeted the guests quietly. He stood on the edge of the circle of men, and she found her way to where the women gathered.

"Tell me, sir," one of the guests began, "is it hard for you to look at us enjoying ourselves? Does your present life pain you?"

Elijah smiled. "Ask my wife. She is the speaker of the family concerning these matters."

Directing his words at the woman, the guest spoke in a loud and brazen voice, "Can you speak of your former happiness and your present misery?"

Orpah remained sitting and answered calmly, "For 50 years the old man and I lived, seeking happiness and never finding it. Now, in our second year here, when we have nothing left, and we live as hired laborers, we have found true happiness. We need nothing more."

The guests all stopped speaking and turned their attention to the old woman, who now stood straight and tall. She smiled at her husband and spoke again. "I speak the truth. We sought happiness for half a century, and while we were rich we never found it. Now that we are poor we are content."

"What makes you happy now?" one of the women asked.

"When we had land and cattle the old man and I never knew a moment's peace. We had no time to talk, to think about our faith, or to pray to God. We had so many worries—how shall we serve the guests, what will people think, will the hired men cheat us? We did not sleep well at night for fear that animals would attack the new calves or robbers would steal the prize horses. We argued over finances, and that is a sin. I thought we should invest one way, and he preferred another."

"And now?"

"Now the old man and I wake in the morning and talk to each other with love and respect. We have nothing to quarrel about, nothing to worry about. Our only concern is to serve the owner well. There is time to talk, to listen, and to pray to God. After 50 years of looking for happiness we have found it."

The guests began to turn away from Orpah and snicker, but Elijah broke in. "Do not laugh, dear friends. My wife and I used to be foolish, and we cried at losing our wealth. God has disclosed a new truth to us, and we share this with you for your own good."

One of the guests broke the long silence and spoke quietly to the old couple. "What you say is simple biblical wisdom. To many people it appeared that you lost the whole world, but actually you have gained your souls."

The Poor Farmer

This story is based on a German folktale, collected by the Grimms.

Once a poor farmer died and went to heaven. When he reached the gates he was seated next to a man who was obviously rich.

In a few moments St. Peter opened the gates and invited the rich man to enter. The farmer peeked through the gates as the two walked into the golden city. What he saw amazed him. A chorus of angels greeted St. Peter and the rich man with a rousing Bach chorale, and people filled the streets shouting. When the noise died down, St. Peter gave a short speech and concluded by saying, "Welcome to the city of God. Make yourself at home." As the rich man walked down the street, people continued to shout and wave.

When it was quiet, St. Peter opened the gates and beckoned to the poor farmer. Though he was greeted warmly there was no angel chorus or great crowds to greet him. "Welcome to the city of God," St. Peter said enthusiastically. "Make yourself at home."

The farmer was deeply hurt. "This is the last place I ever thought I would find discrimination," he said to St. Peter. "All my life I have watched the rich gain privileges that the poor were denied. I thought that when I came to the home of God all would be equal. Yet when I enter the gates I am not greeted by either crowds or choruses."

"My dear friend," St. Peter said, "I can see how it appears that there is discrimination, but it is not true. Everything will be the same for you as for the rich man. You have to understand that today is a special occasion. We receive poor farmers up here every day, but we haven't had a rich man in over 80 years."

The Mountain of the Sun

Like other folktales, a version of this story can be found in many cultures, echoing the words of Jesus, "Do not lay up for yourselves treasures on earth, where moth and rust consume and where thieves break in and steal, but lay up for yourselves treasures in heaven . . ." (Matthew 6:19-20).

A wealthy man died leaving all of his fields and cattle to his two sons. The older brother, not content with half of his father's large fortune, plotted to gain the entire estate.

One day, after the period of mourning had passed, the older brother approached the younger with a proposition. "Let us have a contest," he began. "The one who plows the larger area tomorrow will inherit the entire fortune of our father. There should be one condition: neither of us should eat or drink during the entire day." The younger brother, who greatly admired and trusted his older brother, was quick to accept the proposal.

An hour before dawn the next morning the older brother rose and ate a hearty meal prepared by his wife. Patting his stomach and feeling quite content, he awoke his brother at sunrise. "Be quick, my brother, it is time to begin the contest." Without either eating or drinking the young man raced to the field and began to plow.

During the morning the youth and strength of the younger brother allowed him to race ahead in the contest. By noon, however, the sun began to drain his power. Near midafternoon, thirst and hunger left him weak and faint. At the end of the day the older brother was clearly the winner of the contest. The entire estate of the father was his; the younger brother was a pauper.

Early the next morning the younger brother left home, all of his possessions on his back, in search of a place to work and sleep. He settled in a forest several miles from his father's farm. Each day he cut wood and sold it to people in the neighboring village for a few pennies.

One morning he was about to cut down a tree when a bird flew out of a hole crying with terror. The woodcutter looked into the hole and saw a nest of young birds. "It is not right to cut down the home of these babies," he thought. He found a few soft leaves, laid them in the hole, and proceeded to select another tree. Before he could swing his axe, the mother bird flew to a branch just over his head and spoke. "Thank you for saving the lives of my children," she sang. "I would like to repay you. If you meet me here one hour before sunrise tomorrow with a small sack, I will take you to the Mountain of the Sun where you will find many treasures." Without waiting for a response, she flew away.

Though he was confused by the message of the bird, the young woodcutter arrived at the same spot early the next morning with a small sack. Soon the mother bird appeared. "Come quickly," she sang. "We must leave the mountain before the sun rises." Then off she flew, leading him along a secret path that led straight up the side of a large mountain. When they reached the top he witnessed an amazing sight. On a flat area there was an acre of gold, diamonds, and precious stones.

"Fill your sack and leave before the sun rises," sang the bird. The younger brother responded by quickly filling his small sack with gold, diamonds, and other precious gems. He then thanked the bird and left the Mountain of the Sun. That very day he returned to his hometown where he built a house, bought a field, and married. He soon gained a reputation as a good farmer and a generous man. Life was good for the younger brother.

A few miles to the south the older brother was miserable. Every day people told him about the wealth and generosity of his young-er brother. He could find no rest for his soul until he visited his younger brother and demanded to know how he had gained his wealth. The young farmer, who loved his brother, quickly told him the entire tale, even describing the exact location of the bird's nest

Back at home the older brother paced the floor of his house and thought only of the precious jewels. Finally, taking an axe, he headed for the tree his brother had described. Finding it, he pretended to cut it down. The mother bird flew out of the hole crying loudly. The older brother looked in the hole and said loudly, "Why, look at those pretty babies. I could never cut down this tree, even though it is exactly what I need." He then moved to another tree and swung his axe.

Suddenly the mother bird flew to a branch just over his head and spoke. "Thank you for sparing my children. I would like to repay you. If you meet me here one hour before sunrise tomorrow with a small sack, I will take you to the Mountain of the Sun, where you will find many treasures." Without waiting for a response, she flew away.

The older brother raced home with the exciting news. All night long he and his wife sewed a huge sack out of a bedspread. With dreams of precious gems dancing through his head, he left early in the morning for his meeting with the bird. When the mother bird arrived, she took the older brother along the same secret path to the top of the Mountain of the Sun.

When he saw the size and beauty of the gold and precious stones the older brother fell to his knees shouting for joy. "You must leave before the sun rises," warned the bird. The older brother seemed not to hear as he began to madly fill his sack with gold and diamonds. He ran from one spot to another, shouting each time he placed a jewel in his sack.

"Enough! Enough!" cried the bird. "Run before the sun scorches you with its burning rays!" Then the bird flew away.

Still the older brother continued to fill the sack. When the sun rose, it burned him until he turned into a pile of ashes.

Meanwhile, the younger brother continued to lead a happy and contented life.

The Dog and His Shadow

This is one of Aesop's fables.

A dog was given a fine meaty bone by a friendly neighbor. On his way home, with the bone firmly between his teeth, the animal had to cross a bridge over a narrow stream. When he reached the middle of the bridge the dog paused to look into the water and saw his own reflection magnified. Thinking that the other dog had a larger bone, the animal decided to take it by force. He leaned over and snapped at his own reflection. As he did so, the bone between his teeth fell into the water and was lost.

Fortune and the Poor Man

Based on a folktale collected by the Brothers Grimm.

There was a poor man who complained loudly that the world had been unfair. "Most of those who are rich did nothing to gain their wealth," he cried to anyone who would listen. "They inherit their money from their parents."

One day as the man walked home after expressing his bitter feelings to a crowd at the town square, Fortune appeared before him and said, "I have decided to provide you with wealth. Hold out your purse, and I will fill it with gold coins. There is one condition. If any of the gold falls out of the purse onto the ground, everything I gave you will become dust. Be careful. I see that your purse is old; do not overload it."

The poor man was overjoyed. He opened the strings of his purse and watched as Fortune began to pour a stream of golden coins into it. The wallet soon became heavy.

"Is that enough?" Fortune asked.

"Not yet," the man cried.

Fortune poured several more coins, so that the purse was filled. "Shall I stop?"

"Not yet. Just a few more."

But at that moment the purse split apart, the gold coins fell to the ground, and the treasure turned to dust. Fortune disappeared, and the man was left with an empty wallet.

Three Hundred Gold Coins

". . . for a man's life does not consist in the abundance of his possessions" (Luke 12:15). This story is based on a fable by the famous French writer, Jean De La Fontaine.

There was once a cobbler who was a happy and contented man. People who passed his shop laughed and waved when they saw him singing at the top of his voice while fixing shoes. Many people stopped in his shop just to bask in the warmth of his smile.

One of the people who observed the cobbler was a banker who sang little and smiled less. He seldom slept well. At first he was irritated by the constant good humor of the cobbler, but as the days passed he was attracted to the man. Finally he decided to visit the cobbler and discover his secret of happiness.

After the two men talked for awhile, the banker inquired, "Are you wealthy? Pardon me for asking, but how much money do you make each year?"

"My family is seldom in want," the cobbler answered. "Some days I only fix shoes; no one buys. The shop is closed on holy days, so there is no income at all when we celebrate the witness of a saint. I simply cannot give you an accurate sum."

"How wonderfully simple," the banker said. "I have decided to eliminate your financial problems for the immediate future since you have so openly shared your life story with me. Take this gift of 300 gold coins and use them whenever you have need."

Overjoyed, the cobbler quickly went home and buried the gold in a corner of his house. The succeeding days brought many changes. He often left the shop to go home when the family was absent, thinking that someone might come when they were gone and steal his wealth. He began to lose sleep at night because he feared that people were plotting to steal the gold. Old friends noticed that he did not sing with the same cheer, and he often seemed suspicious when someone stopped in the shop just to chat.

Finally the cobbler visited the banker with the bag of gold in his hands. "Thank you for your generous gift," he began, "but I cannot really afford to be the owner of these gold coins. Please take your money back so that I may again enjoy music, sleep, and my friends. It seems that when I buried the money, I buried happiness at the same time."

The Miser's Pet Bird

The idea for this little story came from a fable by Jonathan Swift.

An old miser kept a tame crow that stole pieces of money and hid them in a hole in the wall. A neighbor's cat watched the antics of the bird and asked, "Why do you hoard those round shiny things that can be of no use to you at all?"

"What I do is no different from my master," said the crow. "He has a whole chest full and makes no more use of them than I."

People are accustomed to be laughed at for their wit, but not for their folly.

The Treasure

I normally avoid using a moral at the end of a fable, but in this one, written by Ivan Kriloff, a 19th-century Russian writer, is so powerful that it sums up the teaching of folk literature regarding greed.

There was a demon who kept watch over a large treasure buried under an old house. One day he was ordered to leave that area for another part of the world. He would not be able to return for 20 years. The demon considered what he should do with the treasure during his absence. Perhaps he should hire a guardian? That would cost a great deal of money. If he left it under the house someone could come and dig it up and steal it. At last a foolproof idea came to him.

He dug up the treasure and took it to the home of a miser. "Dear sir," the demon began, "I wish to give you this gift before I depart for another country. I have always been fond of you, and I pray that you will not refuse my offer. You may feel free to spend it however you desire. When you die, I am to be your sole heir; that is my only stipulation." The miser agreed to accept the gift, and the demon departed.

Twenty years later, having completed his assignment, the demon returned home to find the miser dead from starvation. The demon found the treasure, still intact in the strong box. Not a single coin was missing. He laughed, knowing that the miser had been a guardian who did not cost him a penny.

Is it not true that a miser who hoards his money is merely saving it for the demons?

The Magic Mortar

This Japanese story points to the futility of greed. At the same time it introduces to these pages one of the "Just So" stories, a tale that explains how certain phenomena began. This type of story is evident in Genesis 9:13 and 11:9, explaining the origin of the rainbow and why there are so many languages on earth. In the story of The Magic Mortar *we are told why the ocean is full of salt.*

Long ago two brothers lived in a small village beside the Sea of Japan. The older brother was very wealthy, while the younger brother was quite poor. The day before the end of the year the younger brother went to his older brother's house to borrow some rice.

"We have no rice to begin the new year," he said. "Would you lend me a little? I will repay it as quickly as possible."

"You know I have no rice to spare," said the greedy brother in a gruff voice. "I have just enough for my own family."

Sad and melancholy, the younger brother made his way home. As he walked an old man standing by the side of the road spoke to him. "Why are you so downcast, young fellow?"

"The world is a selfish and heartless place," the younger brother cried. "My own brother won't even lend me rice for the new year."

"All the world is not so bad," the old man assured him. "Take this wheat cake and go to the shrine in the woods. There you will see 20 dwarfs who will ask you for the wheat cake. Don't give it to them unless they give you their stone mortar in exchange."

The younger brother thanked the old man and walked to the shrine in the woods where he saw nearly two dozen dwarfs trying to lift a large log. They shouted and screamed at each other and lifted without success.

"Let me help you," the young man said as he picked up the log and set it easily in the hole."

"You are most kind," the leader of the dwarfs said. Then, spotting the wheat cake, he asked, "What do you have in your hand? It is the most delicious smell in the world!"

"It is a very special wheat cake," the younger brother said softly.

"Please, let us have the wheat cake," the dwarfs said in unison.

"I am sorry," the young man said, "this wheat cake is too precious to me to give away."

Suddenly the dwarfs ran to an old stump and returned with four bags of gold. "We will give you these four bags of gold if you will let us eat the wheat cake."

"I am sorry," the young man said, shaking his head. "I would not trade this wheat cake for all the gold in the world."

Quickly the dwarfs huddled. "It must be a very special wheat cake if he won't trade it for gold," they buzzed.

Turning to the man, they asked, "What do you want for the wheat cake?"

"Well, let me see," he said. "I will trade you this special wheat cake for that stone mortar over by the rock."

Again the dwarfs huddled. In a moment they broke and addressed him. "It is a very special mortar, but we will trade it for your magnificent wheat cake. Be careful," they cautioned. "The mortar is magic. It will give you anything you ask if you turn it to the right. When you have had enough, turn it to the left and it will stop."

The young man thanked the dwarfs and set off whistling with his head held high. Behind him the dwarfs buzzed like a thousand mosquitoes as they devoured the wheat cake. When he got home, the man greeted his wife. "I have something that will end all of our poverty," he said, holding the magic mortar in the air.

"I sent you away for rice and you bring me a stone mortar?" the wife said indignantly.

"This is a hundred times better than a bag of rice," he assured her as he put the mortar on a mat. He gently turned the mortar to the right and said, "Rice, rice, let us have rice." Slowly, steadily, the mortar began to produce beautiful white rice. It soon filled the entire mat. Then, turning the mortar to the left, he said, "Stop!"

Turning to his wife, the man then said, "Bring me two large jugs." When she arrived with the containers, he turned the mortar to the right and whispered, "Wine, wine, let us have wine." Out came pure white wine. "Stop!" he shouted, turning it to the left, and the mortar ceased its production. Both the husband and the wife sipped the wine. It was delicious.

For two hours the couple made a variety of foods for a New Year's Day feast. Finally he decided to ask for something they had always wanted. "House, house, give us a bigger house," he demanded as the mortar turned to the right. Suddenly the building began to move until it spread over a gigantic area. When it finally stopped, they beheld a beautiful mansion, with a lovely garden beside a glistening pond.

The young couple stood together and gazed in wonder at their sudden wealth. They immediately decided to invite their neighbors to a huge celebration. The mortar assisted by making more rice and wine and fish. When the guests arrived in their finest kimonos, the tables of the mansion were piled high with delicious food.

The visitors all wondered about the new wealth of their friends, but no one dared ask about the source of their neighbor's good fortune. The older brother, who had also been invited, was the most puzzled of all. Finally he approached his brother and said, "Yesterday you were at my house asking for a bag of rice, while today you are giving a marvelous feast. What happened?"

The younger brother replied quietly, "I was very fortunate."

Just before the guests were about to leave, the younger brother slipped into the kitchen to make some sweet cakes as a farewell gift to his friends. Turning the magic mortar to the right, he said, "Sweet cakes, sweet cakes, let us have sweet cakes." Little did he know that his older brother was spying on him. When he saw his brother make the first sweet cake, the older brother immediately understood the secret, and went to the garden to consider how he could possess this great gift.

When all the guests had gone, the older brother asked if he might spend the night. "I am not feeling well," he told his younger brother.

A large quilt was found and given to the older brother. He lay on the floor and pretended to go to sleep. When he was certain that all were asleep, he took the magic mortar and headed home. When he came to the sea, he found a little boat on the beach. He pushed the boat from shore, placed the mortar under the seat, and began to row to a nearby island.

As he rowed, his arms began to ache. After an hour he decided to stop and have something to eat. He unwrapped four unsalted rice cakes that he had placed in a bundle. "I wish I had some salt," he thought. Then, looking at the mortar he said out loud, "It is time to test this magic device."

Turning the mortar to the right, he said, "Salt, salt, let us have salt." Slowly the mortar began to produce salt. The man dipped his cake and began to row again as he munched on the rice cake. Meanwhile the mortar continued to make salt in the bottom of the boat. The older brother, unaware that the mortar was still working, soon found the rowing difficult. He then spied the mortar and tried to get it to stop. But he had not observed his brother when he had turned the mortar off.

"Help!" he cried. "The boat will sink." Out in the midst of the dark sea, no one heard him. Soon the waves swamped the boat, drowning the man and sending the mortar to the bottom of the sea. It is said that the mortar is still making salt because no one has turned it to the left. That is why the sea is salty even today.

The Poor Man and the Rich Man

This story is adapted from a German folktale.

One evening as God was traveling the earth on foot, night overtook him before he could find lodging. As he walked a narrow road, two houses appeared before him. One was large and beautiful, the other was small and simple. Assuming that the large house belonged to a wealthy man, the Lord thought, "I will be no burden to the rich man; I'll spend the night with him."

When the rich man opened the door, he looked the traveler over very carefully, from head to toe. "Do you have a room for a stranger?" the Lord asked.

The rich man shook his head slowly. "My rooms are full of expensive furniture and paintings that I am storing until they will bring a good price. Besides, if I opened my door to every beggar who knocked I'd have nothing but rags myself." Having said his piece, the rich man slammed the door shut and left the good Lord standing there.

God turned his back on the house of the rich man and walked across the road to the small house. Before he could speak, the poor man greeted him warmly. "Please spend the night with us. We have a warm bed and plenty to eat."

The wife of the poor man seemed equally pleased that a guest had decided to spend the night. She quickly prepared some vegetables, set the table, and invited the Lord to eat. The food was delicious.

After they drank a cup of coffee and talked, the poor couple insisted that their guest sleep on their bed. Though the Lord did not want to deprive the two old people of their own bed, he found it difficult to refuse. "You have been walking all day," the poor man concluded, "and are very tired."

The next morning when the Lord arose he discovered that the good woman had already been outdoors to milk the cow and had a hot breakfast prepared. After he ate a hearty meal, the Lord thanked the couple and said, "Because you have been so kind and devout, I offer you three wishes. Whatever you ask, I will give you."

The old man was amazed. "We have almost everything we need," he said. "Of course we wish for eternal salvation." He thought a bit and then added, "I wish for good health for both of us and a little daily bread."

God was pleased and said, "Health and a little daily bread are but a single wish. You have one more."

After consulting with his wife, the old man said, "We can't really think of anything else."

"Wouldn't you like a new house in place of this old one?" the Lord inquired.

Together the couple nodded. "That would be nice," the woman responded, speaking for them both. Before the words were out of her mouth, the old hut was gone and a beautiful new home stood in its place. The Lord gave each his blessing and went on.

When the rich man arose that day, he looked out his window and saw his neighbor's new home. Quickly he crossed the road and asked what had happened. Still amazed over their good fortune, the poor couple told the rich man their entire story.

When he returned home and related the tale to his wife, the rich man was angry. "Had I only known that stranger was the Lord I would have at least offered him a place to sleep. If I had not turned him away, we would have had the three wishes."

"It is not too late," his wife cried. "Hurry, fetch a horse and catch him. Invite him to come back and stay with us so that we can have the wishes."

Quickly the rich man saddled a horse and sped off in the direction the Lord had walked. Soon he overtook him. This time the rich man spoke in a polite and kindly fashion, explaining that he had gone to look for bedding but found that the stranger had gone by the time he returned. "If you are ever back in this neighborhood again, I would love to have you stay with me."

The Lord thanked the rich man and assured him that he would stay with him another time if he was ever in the area. Then the rich man asked whether he, too, like his neighbor, might make three wishes.

Gently the Lord told him that he would grant him three wishes but that it would not turn out well for him. "It would be better if you do not use the wishes," the Lord told him.

The rich man assured the Lord that he would pick out something that would be of benefit to himself and his wife. God said, "Go home then, and the three wishes you make will be fulfilled."

As the rich man rode home pondering what great things he might wish for, the horse began to stumble. Irritated, the rich man cried out, "I wish you would break your neck!" Immediately the old horse fell to the ground dead.

Now the rich man had lost his first wish and had to walk home carrying the heavy saddle. As the hot afternoon sun beat down upon him he remembered his wife sitting home in their cool house. The longer he walked, and the hotter the sun became, the more angry he became. Finally, exasperated, he shouted to the sky, "I wish my wife had to sit on this saddle and couldn't get down."

In an instant the saddle vanished, and the man realized his second wish was fulfilled. The last miles seemed just as difficult as the first, even though he did not have to carry the heavy saddle. When he arrived at home he was frustrated at losing his first two wishes and very sore from the long walk.

"Come down from there and fix me a meal," the man shouted when he saw his wife sitting high in the air on the saddle.

"I can't move," she sobbed.

For almost an hour they both struggled to get her down from the saddle. At last, worn out from the work, the rich man was forced to use his third wish to free his wife. In turn for the efforts of the day he got nothing but trouble, a scolding, sore feet, and a dead horse.

The poor couple, however, lived quietly and devoutly until their end.

STORIES OF ANGER AND REVENGE

An Eye for an Eye

Anger easily turns to hatred, which ends in murder. The cross is not only God's answer to the wrath of the Sadducees and the rage of the Pharisees, but also to our anger. If anger is not transformed by love, it becomes a powerful and senseless force, as we see in this story.

In a large town there were two merchants who were fierce competitors. Their stores were across the street from each other. The sole method each man had of determining the success of his business was not daily profit, but how much more business he had than his competitor.

If a customer made a purchase at the store of one merchant, he would taunt his competitor when the sale was complete. The rivalry grew with each succeeding year.

One day God sent an angel to one of the merchants with an offer. "The Lord God has chosen to give you a great gift," the angel said. "Whatever you desire, you will receive. Ask for riches, long life, or healthy children, and the wish is yours. There is one stipulation," the angel cautioned. "Whatever you receive, your competitor will get twice as much. If you ask for 1000 gold coins, he will receive 2000. If you become famous, he will become twice as famous." The angel smiled. "This is God's way of teaching you a lesson."

The merchant thought for a moment. "You will give me anything I request?" The angel nodded. The man's face darkened. "I ask that you strike me blind in one eye."

The Poison Cake

Many years ago in a small hut in a forest in Lithuania there lived a gentle old woman who ate mushrooms and drank water from her private spring. She preferred to be alone, but when she did see people she spoke in proverbs that either baffled or irritated them.

Once, when she saw people dressed in their finest clothes, she said, "A good name is to be preferred to great riches." One day, when a group of children were misbehaving, she addressed their parents, "Train up a child in the way he should go, and when he is old he will not depart from it."

Often the old woman would stop by the home of a rich Polish landlord when she came to town. If she saw him sitting in the sun she would say, "As a door turns on its hinges, so a sluggard turns on his bed." Or she would say, "For lack of wood the fire goes out." Though he often gave her food, he hated the old woman.

One day the woman came upon the lord in the midst of a fierce argument. She moved in between the shouting parties, pointed her finger in the landlord's face, and said, "A hot-tempered man stirs up strife, but he who is slow to anger quiets contention." From that moment the landlord vowed he would get rid of the meddling old woman.

When the woman next visited the rich lord, he baked a beautiful cake full of poison. After talking with her in a friendly fashion, he offered her the present. "You have never tasted cake like this before," he assured her.

Rather than thank him, the old woman whispered again and again, "One day you will find yourself."

As the woman walked down the road, the man muttered to himself, "Today you will find yourself, in the arms of the angel of death."

On the same day that the old woman visited the landlord, his young son participated in a hunt in the woods close to her home. He and his servants lost their way and soon found themselves outside the hut where the old woman lived. The young man knocked on the door and told the woman how hungry and thirsty he was. Immediately she invited him to have a piece of the cake, which had not been touched. The young man fell to the ground dead after the first bite. The servants left immediately to bring the father to his son's side. As he knelt before the body of his son, the tears streaming down the sides of his cheeks, the old woman spoke again, "The man who makes holes falls into them himself."

The Convert

This story is adapted from a Sufi story, collected by Idries Shah.

There was once a convert who had developed a reputation for being a fanatical believer. His vehement attacks on his opponents were known for their anger and harsh rhetoric. One day he explained to a teacher, "For years I worked for the devil full time. Now I work for the Lord full time. I have dedicated my life to opposing everyone whose beliefs are false and who teaches errors. Fighting lies is a full-time job."

The teacher asked the man, "Have you attempted to put yourself in your opponents' positions before you attack them?"

"Indeed I have," replied the convert. "I study them carefully in order to make my charges more devastating. Through study I discover their weaknesses."

Suddenly the mild-mannered teacher exploded. He shouted and pointed his finger at the convert. He called the man names until the convert begged the teacher to stop.

Once again calm and soft spoken, the teacher continued. "In order to put yourself in the place of your opponents, it is not enough to know what they think. You must also know how they feel when you attack them. Only when you fully understand your opponent, intellectually and emotionally, will you be a full servant of the truth."

From that day on the convert was a more humble and thoughtful man.

The Tailor in Heaven

This story is based on a German folktale.

One day the Lord decided to take a long walk in the heavenly garden. In his absence, he left Peter in charge, admonishing him not to admit anyone until he returned. Moments after the Lord left, however, there was a knock at the gate. "Who is there?" Peter demanded.

"I am just a poor honest tailor who begs to be admitted into the presence of the Lord."

"Honest?" Peter asked. "I know your history. You were light fingered and often stole your customer's cloth. I can't let you into the heavenly court anyway, because the Lord has forbidden it while he is gone."

"The only cloth I ever took," protested the tailor, "was little pieces of no value. Have mercy, St. Peter. My feet are blistered from the long journey. Surely you have some work that needs to be done. I'm not proud. I'll do whatever you ask."

Reluctantly Peter allowed the tailor through the gate of heaven, though he told him he would have to sit behind the door in case the Lord would notice him and be angry.

The tailor sat quietly behind the door for a long time. When St. Peter left to run an errand, he decided it was his opportunity to explore. He looked at all of the furniture and peeked into every corner. There were a variety of beautiful chairs that adorned the throne room. In the middle, standing higher than any of the others, was a solid gold armchair with a golden footstool in front of it. It was the chair used by the Lord. The tailor climbed up to the chair and sat down. From that position he could see every place on earth at the same time. It was a tremendous sight.

Suddenly he saw an old woman stealing clothes off a line. The tailor got so angry that he grabbed the golden footstool and threw it at the old woman. When he realized what had happened, and that he couldn't retrieve the footstool, he quickly took his seat behind the door again.

Soon the Lord returned. As he took his seat he didn't see the tailor behind the door, but he immediately missed his footstool. He asked Peter if he had moved it. Peter told him he hadn't touched the footstool. "Did you let anyone in the gate while I was taking my walk?" asked the Lord.

"Only the tailor with blisters on his feet who is sitting behind the door," Peter answered.

Beckoning to the tailor, the Lord asked him, "Where did you put my footstool?"

"My Lord, I know that you will not permit any form of dishonesty," said the tailor. "While I sat on your throne I noticed an old woman stealing dresses off a clothesline. I got so angry with her dishonesty that I threw the footstool at her."

"You miserable rogue," the Lord said firmly. "If I had treated you as you did the woman, what would have happened to you long ago? Besides, I wouldn't have a piece of furniture left in the heavenly court. I deal with sinners primarily through mercy! Get out of my sight. From now on you must stay outside the gate of heaven."

Quickly St. Peter took the tailor outside the gate and left him there. Do you think he is still there, or has the Lord in his mercy allowed him back in?

The Falcon

This story is based on a fable by Leo Tolstoy.

A rich lord had a falcon who he had trained very carefully. It was a splendid bird who was obedient to his master's every command.

One day the lord and a host of his servants went hunting. When the falcon caught his first rabbit, the lord stroked the bird lovingly. Then, being thirsty, he began to search for water. He soon found an old spring on a hillside where the water trickled out of the earth a drop at a time. The lord held his cup under the spring and waited until it was nearly full. As he brought the cup to his mouth, the falcon flapped his wings, spilling the water.

The lord scolded the bird and again placed his cup under the spring. He waited a long time until the cup finally filled. When he began to drink a second time, the falcon landed on his wrist, causing the water to spill on the ground. This time he scolded the bird in a louder voice.

When the lord was able to fill his cup a third time the falcon again caused him to spill the water. The lord became so angry that he struck the bird with all his might, killing it instantly.

This time the lord sent a servant to draw water from the spring. He soon returned with an empty cup. "Sir," he began, "the water is not fit to drink. There is a snake in the spring and it has poisoned the water. If you had drunk the water you would have died."

The lord hung his head. "The falcon saved my life, and in anger I killed him for it," he said weeping.

STORIES OF FRIENDSHIP AND FIDELITY

Companions of the King

"A good story in Hasidic Judaism is not about miracles, but about friendship and hope—the greatest miracles of all."—Elie Wiesel

There were two men who were inseparable friends from childhood. Though their love bound them together, a series of unfortunate circumstances forced them to live in separate and hostile countries. One day one of the men, a merchant, came to visit his friend. The king was informed that a stranger from an enemy country was walking the streets of his capital, and the man was arrested immediately. After a brief trial the king ordered the executioner to remove his head.

The merchant fell to his knees and begged the king to allow him to complete his business before he was killed. "Your majesty, all my money is invested with other merchants, and we have no written documents," he cried. "If I die without clearing my financial affairs, my wife and children will be destitute. Permit me to go home and set my business in order and I will return."

"Do you take me for a fool?" the king demanded. "Who has ever heard of a prisoner returning without force?"

"Your majesty," the man replied, "I have a friend in your country who will be security for me."

The king ordered the friend to his court and asked, "Will you be security for your companion? Understand that if he does not return you will die!"

"I count it an honor to offer my life as security for my closest friend," the man replied. The king was astonished and allowed the merchant one month to finish his business. "If you do not return in 30 days we will cut off the head of your companion."

On the last day of the month the king waited until dusk for the merchant to return. Just before the sun was to set the king ordered the executioner to remove the head of the prisoner. As the man knelt before the great wooden block, there was a shout from those assembled. "The merchant is coming!"

As the man arrived he saw that his friend was about to be slain. Quickly he moved to the execution block and pushed his friend aside gently. "I am ready to assume my punishment," he said, kneeling.

The other man was not easily convinced. "I am ready to die in your place," he said firmly. The two men argued for several minutes, each declaring his intention to be the one who would be executed. Meanwhile the king and his court watched the discussion with amazement.

Finally the king ordered the sword to be removed, saying, "I have never witnessed such devotion in all my life. Both of you are pardoned!"

Next the king called the two men before him. "Deep friendship is a rare jewel," the king said simply. "I beg you, allow me to join you as a third." From that day on the two men became companions of the king.

The Inheritance

This story is based on a Jewish folktale.

There was once a man who promised to give all 10 of his children 100 gold coins on the day of his death. At the time that he made the promise, the man had far more than the promised amount. In his last days, however, he fell on hard times. He soon found that he was short of the money needed to keep his word to all his children.

On the day of his death, the children gathered beside their father's bed at his request. One by one they stepped forward, embraced their father, and received a purse with 100 gold coins. When it was time for the youngest son to be paid, the father waved everyone out of the room.

"My son," the dying man began, "I have terrible news. Though I have been able to give each of your brothers and sisters 100 gold coins, I have but 20 for you."

"Father," the youngest child protested, "if you knew this why did you not make adjustments with all of your children?"

"It is better that I keep my word to as many as possible," the father said. "Although I cannot give you as many gold coins as I promised, I can give you my greatest treasure. In addition to the 20 coins which I have for you, I offer you my 10 closest companions. Their friendship is worth more than all the gold I have ever possessed. I urge you to treat them kindly." Shortly after he spoke, the man died.

When the period of mourning was over, the nine oldest children, thrilled by their sudden wealth, left for an extended vacation. The youngest child remained home, deeply disappointed. When he paid off his debts he found he had only four coins remaining. Though he had no great desire to see his father's friends, he decided he must honor his beloved father's last request. Reluctantly he spent the remaining portion of his inheritance and invited the 10 companions to dinner.

When the meal was over, the old men said to one another, "This is the only child who treats us with kindness. Let us return his affection."

The next morning each of his father's 10 friends sent two cattle and a small purse of money to the youngest son. Several of the old men provided assistance in breeding the cattle. Soon the youngest child had a large herd. Others offered advice on how to invest money. It was not long before the youngest son had greater wealth than any of the other nine. Above his desk he wrote these words: "Friendship is of more value than gold."

The Rabbi's Disgrace

There was once a rabbi who preached powerful sermons in the synagogue on Friday evenings. A certain woman came each Sabbath to listen. She was so enchanted with his voice and his message that she sat meditating long after the sermon was over. One night when she returned home, her husband demanded, "Where have you been? The sermon was over long ago!"

The woman answered truthfully, "I was so caught up with the sound of the rabbi's voice that I stayed until the Sabbath light went out."

Each week for several months the same conversation took place. Finally, in anger, the husband shouted, "I will not speak to you again until you spit in the rabbi's face!"

The woman thought her husband's anger would soon die out, but when he did not return home for two days she became greatly distressed. Though she loved her husband very much, she could never do anything that would bring dishonor to her rabbi. She shared her problem with her two closest friends, who went to visit the rabbi.

Two days later the woman and her two friends were called to the office of the rabbi. When they arrived they found the great man sitting with his head in his hands, his eyes closed. "I am in great pain," said the rabbi. "My eyes have gone bad. I have called you because it has been revealed to me that healing can only take place through the prayers and powers of righteous women. Please pray for me!"

In earnest the three women began to pray. After a few moments the rabbi said, "It has also been revealed to me that the pain in my head can only be removed if a woman of faith spits seven times in my eyes. Would the woman who spends the most time in the synagogue perform the cure for me?"

The woman's two companions both turned to her, indicating that she was the one to perform the cure. Obediently the woman moved in front of the rabbi and spit seven times in his eyes. When she was finished the rabbi opened his eyes and smiled. "Go home and tell your husband that not only have you spit once in the rabbi's face, but that you have spit seven times."

When his disciples heard what had happened, they confronted him angrily. "You have brought dishonor on the Torah and those who study it! How could you shame your name and the office of rabbi?"

The teacher replied, "Compared to the value of a marriage, my name is nothing. I am proud to do so little to bring peace between a husband and wife."

The Wooden Bowl

"Honor your father and mother" was not originally so much about children sassing their parents as about providing respect and care for older people. Given this understanding, this German folktale is a commentary on the Fourth Commandment.

There was once a couple who lived with their only son Conrad in a modest house at the edge of a great forest. Though they were not rich, they lived a comfortable and happy life together.

One day the man's father came to make his home with the young couple. The old grandfather's eyes had grown dim, his ears nearly deaf, and his hands shook like leaves in the wind. When he ate he was unable to hold his spoon without spilling food on the tablecloth and the floor. Often bits of food would run out of his mouth, soiling his clothing. For months the young couple discussed the irritating behavior of the old man. Finally they set a table for him to eat in a corner of the kitchen. As he ate, he looked sadly at his family. When he spilt his food, he would sob.

Finally one day the old man's trembling hands could no longer hold the glass bowl, and it fell to the floor, breaking into a dozen pieces. The woman scolded him and immediately went to the market where she purchased a wooden bowl for the grandfather. As the days passed the old man said very little as he sat in his corner eating out of his wooden bowl.

Late in the fall the father came home from a long day's work to find Conrad sitting in the middle of the floor carving a block of wood. "What are you making, my young man?" asked the father.

"It is a present for you and mommy," answered the child. "I am carving two wooden bowls so that you will have something to eat from when you live with me in your old age."

The husband and wife looked at each other for a long time, and finally they began to weep. That evening they moved the old grandfather back to the family table. From that day on he always ate with them, and they said nothing even when he spilled his food.

The Wolf and the Cat

In this story, adapted from a fable by Ivan Kriloff, we witness the sense of cause and effect that is a trademark of most folk literature. The concluding biblical verse could well be the theme of many fables: "Whatever a man sows, that he will also reap" (Galatians 6:7).

A wolf fled from the forest into a village in great fear. The huntsmen and a pack of hounds were after him. He looked desperately for an opening in the city's walls but found that every gateway was closed.

Looking up on the wall the wolf saw a cat and cried, "My good friend, tell me quickly which of the neighboring farmers is the kindest. I desperately need shelter." As he spoke, the barking of the dogs drew nearer.

"Go quickly and ask old Peter at the north end of the village," the cat replied. "He is a kind and generous man."

"That is true," said the wolf, "but I recently tore the skin off one of his sheep."

"Well," the cat said slowly, "you could try Hans on the west side of the village."

"I am afraid that he is angry with me too," the wolf said slowly. "I carried off one of his kids."

"Then run to the south. Halvor's farm is not far away."

"Halvor is still upset from last spring. He has threatened me over one of his lambs."

"There is really only one other possibility," the cat concluded. "Daniel's farm is just on the other side of the woods."

"I don't think Daniel is the best choice. I killed one of his calves two weeks ago."

"My dear friend," the cat said from the safety of his perch, "it is obvious that you have made enemies of the most patient farmers in our area. None of these men have lost their senses. They wish to see you dead, and you have only yourself to blame. The Good Book says, "Whatever a man sows, that he will also reap.""

A Thief in the Night

Like the last story, this fable is also based on a work by the Russian writer Ivan Kriloff.

A thief crept into a farmer's house one night and emptied his storeroom. When the farmer awoke in the morning, he discovered he had lost everything he owned that had great value. Weeping and wailing, he called together all of his friends and relatives.

"Help me in my time of great trouble," he cried.

The first neighbor sighed and said, "It was not wise of you to boast to all how rich you have become."

A second neighbor stepped forward. "In the future you must be more careful and lock your storeroom securely."

One of the relatives now spoke. "What you must do is to protect your valuables with guard dogs. Surely you will be able to find animals as brave as my dogs who will run off any thieves who come to you in the night."

After listening to dozens of pieces of advice from his loving friends and relatives, the man went into his house and wept. Though people had been free with words of counsel, not a single person had offered to help the poor fellow.

The Most Precious Gift

There was a poor landless peasant who lived alone in a hut with his daughter. One day, through an edict of the king, he received a small parcel of land where he could grow food. As the peasant prepared the field, his hoe struck a hard object. When he cleared off the dirt he discovered a gold mortar. Immediately he rushed home and showed it to his daughter.

"I have decided to offer the gold mortar to the king, as a way of thanking him for his gift of land," said the man.

"Father," the daughter cautioned, "I think you should reconsider your decision. Rather than be grateful for the gift, the king will suspect that you are withholding the pestle. I think you should keep quiet about the gold mortar."

The peasant, however, would not listen to his daughter's advice. He immediately left for the palace and requested an audience with the king. "I present this gold mortar to you as a token of my fidelity and respect," said the peasant. "I discovered it in the field you recently gave me."

"Something is missing," said the king after he examined the gold object carefully. "Where is the pestle?"

"I dug the mortar out of the earth, my lord," said the peasant. "I did not find a gold pestle."

The king did not believe the peasant and threw him into prison until he produced the pestle. The farmer was so upset that he refused to eat. All day long he cried, "If only I had listened to my daughter."

Afraid that the peasant might become sick, the king's servants reported to their master. "All day long he cries, 'If only I had listened to my daughter.'"

Puzzled by the words of the peasant, the king called for him and asked why he continually spoke of his daughter. "She warned me not to bring the mortar. She said that you would demand the pestle, which I did not find. She is brilliant and wise. I should have listened to her advice."

Intrigued by the story, the king asked to meet the young woman. When she arrived at the castle he spoke with her and asked her questions. He was impressed by her clever answers. To test her quick mind he proposed a riddle. "If you can find an answer I will marry you."

"And what is the riddle, my lord?" asked the peasant's daughter.

"Come to me neither clothed nor naked, neither riding nor driving, neither on the road nor off the road. This is the riddle," said the king.

The woman bowed and immediately left the castle. She took off all her clothes, and thus was unclothed. She then wrapped a fish net around herself so that she was no longer naked. She borrowed a donkey and tied the fish net to the donkey's tail. She had the donkey drag her in the net. Thus she was neither riding nor driving. In addition, the donkey had to drag her in a rut, so that she touched the ground with only her big toe. She was neither on the road nor off the road. When she arrived, the king was astounded, and he immediately released her father from prison and asked for her hand in marriage.

As the years passed the queen developed a reputation for being compassionate and wise. Many believed that she was superior to her husband in intelligence. People also believed that the king was irritated when the queen demonstrated her quick mind.

One day the king was asked to settle a dispute between two farmers over the ownership of a young foal that had run away and lain down between two cows. The first man said, "The foal clearly belongs to me. I can produce the young horse's mother." The king, however, ruled that the foal belonged to the man who owned the cows, though it was clear that it should not belong to him.

The true owner of the horse was greatly troubled at the king's ruling. One day he spotted the queen taking a walk and told her his story, appealing to her for mercy. Listening carefully, the queen said to the owner of the horse, "I will tell you what to do, but you must never reveal where you received the idea. You will need a fishing pole and a large net." She then whispered the plot to the man.

When the king took his daily tour of the city the next day he saw a curious sight. In the middle of the town square, on dry land, he saw the owner of the horse pretending to fish. "Whatever are you doing?" the king asked the horse's owner.

"I am fishing," came the prompt reply.

"But there is no water for over a mile," the king protested.

"I can fish on dry land as surely as a cow can have a foal," answered the man in a loud voice for all to hear.

"Who put you up to this?" the king demanded. "I do not appreciate being humiliated in the middle of the town square." The man protested that it was his own idea. Finally, under great pressure, he revealed that the queen had given him the plan.

Immediately the king returned to the palace and confronted his wife. "Why did you publicly humiliate me? This is not the first time you have demonstrated your cleverness to my discredit. I no longer want you for my wife. I will give you 24 hours to get out of the palace." The king then stomped out of the room.

In an hour he returned a bit more calm. "In order that you do not have to live in poverty you may take whatever is most precious to you in the palace."

The queen threw her arms around her husband and cried, "I love you with all my heart. I don't want to leave you, but if you insist I will do whatever you ask."

That night the queen ordered the finest wine from the king's cellar and mixed it with a strong sleeping potion. She asked the king to join her for a farewell drink. When the king put the cup to his lips, he immediately fell into a deep sleep. The queen called her servant, who wrapped the king in a large linen cloth and carried him to a waiting carriage. The carriage drove to the home of her father, where the servant placed the king into a large bed.

When he awoke the next morning, the king was angry. "You have abducted me with the help of my own servants," he shouted.

Standing before her husband, the queen said softly, "When you ordered me to leave, you told me to take whatever was most precious to me. I did. You are the dearest and most precious gift of all, and the only thing I care about in the entire palace."

Tears came to the eyes of the king. "My dear wife," he said, taking her into his arms, "I love you. Stay with me forever." And she did.

Abraham and Mary

Many years ago a group of holy men went to the desert to pray and learn to be totally dependent on God. In an age when people judged success only by the amount of things they acquired, the

Desert Fathers, as they were called, offered an alternative life-style, and so began a reform movement in the church.

One of the men who made his home in the wilderness was Abraham or, as he was known to some, Abba Abraham. For nearly 50 years Abraham ate neither bread nor meat. His life was simple and quiet.

One day his only brother died and left a young daughter, Mary, an orphan. Abba Abraham adopted Mary and housed her in the outer room of his cell. Through the small window between the two rooms, Abraham taught Mary the Psalms and other passages of Scripture. She eagerly prayed and sang with her uncle and even abstained from eating meat and rich food as he did. For 20 years Mary lived with Abraham in full devotion to God.

One day a monk, perhaps a monk in name only, came to visit Abraham for edification. He was overcome with desire for Mary and began to speak tenderly to her. She had never known the attention of a man and was flattered by his advances. After many months of quiet conversation, she left her cell and walked alone with him. In the heat of passion they came together, but when the deed was done, she trembled with guilt. Weighed down with anguish, she felt as if she had shamed her uncle, herself, and her God.

Silently, without speaking to anyone, she left for another city, taking refuge in a brothel.

Abraham was greatly grieved when he discovered that Mary had left. In prayer it was revealed to him that his niece was living a wanton life. After two years he discovered where she was and exactly what she did. He sent a friend to go to the brothel and return with as much information as possible.

When the friend returned, Abraham developed a plan to bring Mary back. He disguised himself as an army officer and went to the inn where she worked. The normally quiet monk swaggered into the main room of the inn and bellowed, "I hear you have a fine young wench here. Let me have a look at her." When they were introduced, the blessed Abraham nearly dissolved in grief to see her clothed in a harlot's dress. Disguising his grief, he said in a loud voice, "I've come a long way for the love of Mary!"

Abraham invited the woman to join him for a huge meal. Though his stomach had not tasted meat or most of the other foods for nearly 50 years, he ate and drank with gusto. When the meal was over, the young girl invited him to come up to her room to lie with her.

Once upstairs, Mary knelt to untie his shoes. Speaking softly, the old monk said, "I've come a long way for the love of Mary." Immediately she recognized her dear uncle.

At first she resisted the old man's invitation to return to their home. "I cannot even look at you," she cried. "I am so full of shame."

Then Abba Abraham told his beloved niece stories of Christ forgiving and freeing an unclean woman who later repaid him by washing his feet with her hair and her tears. He told other powerful stories, and through them Mary remembered the great redeeming love of the Savior. But of even more importance to her was the action of her uncle. She realized what a great sacrifice he had made to break his vow. She knew how much he loved her, and through that love she could imagine God's love for her.

She returned to the desert that day to resume her life of prayer and meditation. She provided inspiration, counsel, and understanding to all who visited her cell. There were no sins she could not understand. After her death she became known as St. Mary the Harlot.

BIBLIOGRAPHY

Adams, Richard. *Watership Down.* London: Rex Collings, Ltd., 1972.

Aesop's Fables. Based on a translation by George Fyler Townsend. Garden City: Doubleday, 1968 (out of print; other editions available).

Ausubel, Nathan, ed. *A Treasury of Jewish Folklore: Stories, Traditions, Legends, Humor, Wisdom and Folk Songs of the Jewish People.* New York: Crown, 1948.

Chesterton, G. K. *All Things Considered.* Freeport, New York: Books for Libraries Press, 1971 (First published 1908).
   His essay on the moral nature of what he calls fairy stories is delightful; c.f., p. 253.

Coerr, Eleanor. *Sadako and the Thousand Paper Cranes.* New York: Putnam's, 1977.
   This illustrated book tells the story of Sadako very simply.

Doberstein, John W. "Luther and the Fables of Aesop." *The Lutheran Church Quarterly.*

Gerbner, George. "TV's Changing Our Lives." *Presbyterian Survey* (January 1982), pp. 11ff.

Gerbner, George. "Television As Religion." *Media and Values* 17 (Fall 1981), pp. 1-3.

Greeley, Andrew M. *The Religious Imagination.* New York: William H. Sadler, Inc., 1981.

    In this sociological study of the faith of Roman Catholic young adults, Fr. Greeley concludes that it is necessary for us to use storytelling in education. Chapter 19 is the place where he makes his storytelling observations.

The Grimms' German Folk Tales. Translated by Francis P. Magoun Jr. and Alexander H. Krappe. Carbondale: Southern Illinois University Press, 1960.

    Over 200 of the stories collected by Jacob and Wilhelm Grimm are in this book. The reader who is only familiar with the polished children's editions will be delighted and surprised by the power and diversity of folktales.

Hauerwas, Stanley. *A Community of Character: Toward a Constructive Christian Social Ethic.* Notre Dame: University of Notre Dame Press, 1981.

    Part 1 of Prof. Hauerwas's book is entitled, "The Narrative Character of Christian Social Ethics." I have used a great deal of his work in formulating my notion of true stories and their impact on the lives and characters of people. My opening chapter has also borrowed from his initial essay, "A Story-Formed Community: Reflections on *Watership Down.*"

Komroff, Manuel. *The Great Fables of All Nations.* New York: Tudor Publishing Company, 1928.

    In addition to familiar fables by Aesop, this 487-page book has fables by Jonathan Swift, Jean De La Fontaine, Benjamin Franklin, Christian Gellert, Leo Tolstoy, and nearly 25 other authors.

Lane, Belden C. "Rabbinical Stories: A Primer on Theological Method." *The Christian Century* (December 16, 1981), pp. 1306ff.

    In this article Prof. Lane makes a distinction between *haggadah* and *halakah* and gives story examples of the *haggadic* method.

Newsweek, (December 6, 1982), pp. 136-140.

    This is an article on the impact of television.

Noy, Dov, ed. *Folktales of Israel,* Chicago: The University of Chicago Press, 1963.

    This is an extremely helpful book. It is a collection of oral, not written, stories told by Jewish people who have settled in Israel.

Shah, Idries. *The Magic Monastery.* New York: E. P. Dutton and Co., 1972.

    Idries Shah is a prolific writer who introduces us to the Sufi stories, religious tales coming out of the Islamic tradition.

Tolstoy, Leo. *The Short Stories of Leo Tolstoy.* New York: Bantam, 1960 (out of print).

    Most of these stories come from Tolstoy's later years, when he was attempting to write on religious subjects. He has re-shaped old Russian folktales, as well as created his own stories. Often they begin with a biblical text.

Uchida, Yoshiko. *The Magic Listening Cap: More Folk Tales from Japan.* New York: Harcourt, Brace and World, Inc., 1955.

    The Magic Mortar, a story I first heard Jay O'Callahan tell, is just one of the many fine tales found in this collection.

White, William R. *Speaking in Stories.* Minneapolis: Augsburg, 1982.

    This book is a resource for Christian storytelling.

Wiesel, Elie. *Messengers of God: Biblical Portraits and Legends.* New York: Random House, 1976.

The stories Wiesel includes, plus the comments he makes on biblical figures, make this a valuable resource.

Wiesel, Elie. *Souls on Fire: Portraits and Legends of Hasidic Masters.* New York: Random House, 1972.

This book provides us with stories from a group of passionate Jews whose theology moved by story.

Wilde, Oscar. *The Happy Prince and Other Stories.* New York: Penguin, 1962.

Wood, A. Skevington. *The Burning Heart: John Wesley, Evangelist.* London: The Paternoster Press, 1967.